C A P S T O N E

D1311093

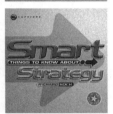

Stay Smart!

Smart things to know about... is a complete library of the world's smartest business ideas. **Smart** books put you on the inside track to the knowledge and skills that make the most successful people tick.

Each book brings you right up to speed on a crucial business issue. The subjects that business people tell us they most want to master are:

*Smart Things to Know about **Brands & Branding**,* JOHN MARIOTTI

*Smart Things to Know about **Business Finance**,* KEN LANGDON

*Smart Things to Know about **Change**,* DAVID FIRTH

*Smart Things to Know about **Customers**,* ROS JAY

*Smart Things to Know about **E-Commerce**,* MIKE CUNNINGHAM

*Smart Things to Know about **Influencing Skills**,* NICOLA PHILLIPS

*Smart Things to Know about **Knowledge Management**,* TOM M. KOULOPOULOS

*Smart Things to Know about **Strategy**,* RICHARD KOCH

*Smart Things to Know about **Teams**,* ANNEMARIE CARACCIOLO

You can stay **Smart** by e-mailing us at **capstone_publishing@msn.com**. Let us keep you up to date with new Smart books, Smart updates, a Smart newsletter and Smart seminars and conferences. Get in touch to discuss your needs.

Smart Things to Know about Change

CAPSTONE

Smart

THINGS TO KNOW ABOUT

Change

DAVID FIRTH

Copyright © David Firth 1999

The right of David Firth to be identified as the author of this work has been asserted in accordance with the Copyright, Designs and Patents Act 1988

First published 1999 by

Capstone USA
LPC Group
40 Commercial Park
Milford
CT 06460
USA

Capstone Publishing Limited
8, Newtec Place,
Magdalen Road,
Oxford OX4 1RE
United Kingdom
http://www.capstone.co.uk

Reprinted 2000 (twice)

British Library Cataloguing in Publication Data
A CIP catalogue record for this book is available from the British Library

ISBN 1-84112-035-9

Typeset by
Sparks Computer Solutions, Oxford
http://www.sparks.co.uk
Printed and bound by
T.J. International Ltd, Padstow, Cornwall

This book is printed on acid-free paper

for Margie

Contents

What is Smart?

The *Smart* series is a new way of learning. *Smart* books will improve your understanding and performance in some of the critical areas you face today like *customers, strategy, change, e-commerce, brands, influencing skills, knowledge management, finance, teamworking, partnerships.*

Smart books summarize accumulated wisdom as well as providing original cutting-edge ideas and tools that will take you out of theory and into action.

The widely respected business guru Chris Argyris points out that even the most intelligent individuals can become ineffective in organizations. Why? Because we are so busy working that we fail to learn about ourselves. We stop reflecting on the changes around us. We get sucked into the patterns of behavior that have produced success for us in the past, not realizing that it may no longer be appropriate for us in the fast-approaching future.

There are three ways the *Smart* series helps prevent this happening to you:

- by increasing your self-awareness

- by developing your understanding, attitude and behavior

- by giving you the tools to challenge the status quo that exists in your organization.

Smart people need smart organizations. You could spend a third of your career hopping around in search of the Holy Grail, or you could begin to create your own smart organization around you today.

Finally a reminder that books don't change the world, people do. And although the *Smart* series offers you the brightest wisdom from the best practitioners and thinkers, these books throw the responsibility on you to *apply* what you're learning in your work.

Because the truly smart person knows that reading a book is the start of the process and not the end ...

As Eric Hoffer says, 'In times of change, learners inherit the world, while the learned remain beautifully equipped to deal with a world that no longer exists.'

David Firth
Smartmaster

Preface

Change: It's All Been a Big Misunderstanding

'God, grant me the serenity to accept the things I cannot change, the courage to change the things I can, and the wisdom to know the difference.'

The 'serenity' prayer, Reinhold Niebuhr

'Everything is in transition. Nothing is permanent except this. Change is a force you have to groove with, not resist. Like a fast and furious monster of epic proportions, it charges headlong into the deep unknown with you clinging on to its back. You can't get off, because it's going too fast. It can't stop, because constant movement is all it knows. Give yourself up to the ride and, with the belief that all things work together for the good say: "All change is good, all change is good, all change is good, all change is good, all change is good, all change is good, all change is good, all change is good, all change is good, all change is good, all change is good."'

Barefoot Doctor's *Handbook for the Urban Warrior*

'Wouldn't it be better if I just went home to bed?'

Ebenezer Scrooge, *A Christmas Carol*

The great thing about change is that it's one of the few work-related issues that you can talk about quite happily and productively with your family and friends. No-one is going to thank you at the George & Dragon if you strike up a conversation about strategy or process redesign (honestly they won't, so don't even try it). But bring up change and you'll draw people in. Your Grandma will tell you about how much easier things were when they were all made of wood, and manners were better. And talking about change with your friends gets them to talk gleefully about all the myriad reversals that have impacted their life since last you saw them – babies conceived, championships lost, jobs won, habits broken, moral, legal and psychological battles fought. Everyone knows, if not loves, change. And everyone knows – at some conscious level – that change is *the* colorful, frustrating, multi-patterned, life-bringing rhythm of life. That's one of the reasons that this book has such a slant towards the people-related aspects of change.

In the business world though, change is talked about in almost reverential terms. Change in business has a capital C. Change in business is (voice shifts to apocalyptic, hushed tone) *Very Serious Indeed*.

And you can perhaps understand why. We live in an age of vast social transformation equal in power and scope to the Renaissance and Industrial Ages. When you realize that these three ages – Renaissance, Industrial, Information (or whatever term you apply to the present one) have occurred in the last blink of an eye of man's existence on this planet, you can accept that humanity is learning to accelerate the natural cycles of being born, growth, maturity, decline, death and rebirth. Our tool of choice, the computer, doubling its processor speed every six months, almost guaranteeing technological obsolescence as soon as we've unpacked the box, drives us to work, learn and live faster and faster. Speed is the late 20th Century drug of choice. Everything speeds, including change.

Change is a Very Big Thing

You'd think change was the worst thing to happen to business. A disaster. The Smart Change Master needs to work against this conditioning.

Take any volume from the business-change literature down from the shelf and it's doom and gloom time. We read about the enormity of the change task. We read about the relentless pressures facing the modern organization. And at the personal level, what do you hear about people? Are they skipping and singing that their company's going through another change? Are they up for it, willing, capable? No. People resist change. They fear change. They do – the ungrateful bastards. So they need pushing and pulling and pummeling and pampering (in the words of Robbins and Finley). They need to be made to change, or else they'd just hang around with an empty expression on their faces, breathing up the CEO's oxygen.

Honestly, I don't know if you know any of these People in Change Books, or if you work alongside any at your place, but it makes me wonder how they ever got jobs in these prestigious case study companies. People in Change Books – contrary, difficult, unpredictable, needy, weak – remind me of that cartoon character in *Viz*, the British comic: Miss Jelly Head. Poor girl, no brain. She used to just lay around staring blankly out of the page whilst unfeasibly silly events unfolded about her – bank robberies, assassinations, runaway steam rollers. 'If only Miss Jelly Head could reach the brake!' But she couldn't, of course, because she had no brain. Totally useless, just like a Person in a Change Book.

If your People are PCBs like that – contrary, difficult, unpredictable, needy, weak – then read no further, because this isn't a manual for dealing with sociopaths. Nothing here will work on people like that. Best thing you could do is have a word with your HR department and ask them why they're recruiting the dregs of the employment market. And ask your head-hunter/recruitment consultant where he goes on holiday.

I believe one of the things that makes change such a serious thing in organizations is a commonly accepted assumption about people – namely that they are contrary, difficult, unpredictable, needy and weak. I have a

---

CHANGE IS A BIG THING FOR ORGANIZATIONS BECAUSE:

- 'they'll' resist it
- major disruption is going to happen, which will cost us money
- change is complex in large organizations and just thinking about doing it will take up lots of our already over-stretched time. Not thinking about it enough will cost us even more
- we're not very good at it, on a personal or group level
- it's not clear whether the unknown future might turn out to be worse than the present known
- we're just not sure
- even if we do OK with this change, we just know there'll be another one coming soon
- change initiatives in organizations like ours have produced job losses, anger, resentment, higher stress, loss of trust, confusion and has brought out some of the darker sides of peoples' nature – deceit, guilt, envy, hatred. Why on Earth would we bother to do it again?

and, biggest thing of all,

- we'd much prefer if it weren't happening.

---

more optimistic faith in the potential of human beings. I believe if you look for weakness and fear, you'll find it. I believe if you expect support, feedback, creativity and willingness, you'll create it.

This does not mean that in my world people do not behave cynically and negatively – these are fairly common human traits, and I'm surprised when people are so hurt when they find them displayed. But in my ideal organization, a leader would want to take the time to understand *why* people were behaving like that, and find out *what* could be done to help them leave those unhelpful behaviors behind. Now *that's* smart ...

What's the Big Thing about change?

OK. Some smart self-awareness time!

Nature has no problem with change. The seasons come and go, always. Over the vast plains of the millennia, a myriad species evolve, adapt, survive or die, fly, creep, crawl, lumber, swing, fly, swim, become fuel. Down under the earth, the deep plates shift and grind. The planet farts a volcano here, shakes an earthquake there, heats up, cools down, balances out, supports life. From the Earth's perspective (4.65 billion years and counting), there is time to change, time to experiment, time to sort things out.

For Mankind, on the other hand, compressed into our little time capsules of 70 or 80 years, change is a good degree or two more difficult and complex. However, time, or the lack of it, is not really the problem. After all, we've all got the same amount of time, yes, we've all got the same number of hours in the day to work with.

So what makes the difference? We've got our Ego, and with it comes a whole catalog of fears and shadows (not having enough time is just another Ego excuse generated by facing dilemmas that leave us exposed. If you say that you don't have enough time, you are apparently excused from doing the important things first).

In the business world, Change is Very Serious Indeed because it's assumed that people are naturally afraid of change. That's nonsense; our fears are much more specific than that – and they are all Ego driven. We're fearful of not living up to our own expectations, even more afraid of not living up to the expectations of others. We're scared of not really knowing what we want or what we're really supposed to be doing with our lives. We're scared of the implications of finding out. We're scared of losing our status, our reputation, our knowledge, the currency of our skills, our influence. We're scared of being found out. We're scared of who we are and who we might become, were we not so full of being who we are. We're scared of losing our job, our hair, our figure, our teeth, our traveller's checks, our marketability, our income, our home, our holiday entitlement which should by rights be carried over from last year, our sex life. Our minds. So we keep busy. We've got lots to do, to keep our fears at bay. Our personal organizers shadow us. We're scared of losing our personal organizers.

We have much to admit to being afraid of before we can say that we are scared of change.

So change gets a bad press, at both the personal and organizational levels, because whilst it promises happiness, it can also bring sadness; because it promises joy, but can also bring pain; and because, whilst it offers progress, it also threatens everything that has previously brought us satisfaction. And the Ego thrives on this fear.

Meanwhile, whether we worry or not, change pulses like the energy it is through our lives.

You embody change. Whilst you are reading this book, your cells will die away and be replaced a million times. Your blood will be muddied and cleansed with every breath. Your hair will fall about you and catch in the keys of your PC. Your nails will grow, imperceptibly, inexorably. In your external environment, change pulses and flows. Events occur, some shaped by you, most not. Things change, you adapt, you learn, just as you always have. People do change, happily and effectively. You used to shit in your pants.

But many things don't turn out as we expect, many things don't happen in the way we plan. Some things turn up unexpectedly, sometimes. Like death.

We cannot predict the future, we cannot guarantee anything. We do not always get what we want.

So *there's a great deal we can't do about change*. Sometimes acceptance may be the real answer, and not change.

Smart quotes

'You can't have everything. Where would you put it?'

Steven Wright

Let's be real about change

The stress that is often reported around change happens because we want both to predict the future and to guarantee results. It's a control thing. It is one of the seductions of the Ego that we could live a life of ease and contentment if we could get what we want. And that means guaranteeing the future. When we fail at this impossible task, we taunt ourselves with 20/20 hindsight, 'should-haves' and 'ought-to-haves'. Next time, we assure ourselves, we'll be better at predicting *everything*.

Why do we go along with the Ego in enjoying this silly fantasy? Fear, perhaps. At base, the fear that we won't be up to it if things don't turn out as we hope. The fantasy of believing that we'll be able to control all change is less painful than the possibility that we might be found wanting if we drop the façade.

And because when one thing changes, everything changes – all futures shift – our need to control is doubly mocked. It's not just that we can't guarantee the future, we also can't possibly keep up to all that is happening. Change unfolds life before us, domino paths of possibility and chance scattering messily away into the distance, when really what we'd most like to do is get it all tidied up and put away.

All spiritual teachings tell you to accept what you cannot change. The business world doesn't like that idea.

The futility of attempting to control change has not sunk in to the business world. We can say the words 'change is a constant' to each other as if we believe it , but we really have not grasped the omnipotence and omnipresence that this description confers on it. Change in business is just another annoying thing, like human beings, to be managed. Failure to do so is always accompanied by recrimination, and more funding for an even more (less?) effective Project Management methodology. Change, in business, is still pretty much A Bad Thing rather than The Only Thing.

Smart quotes

'It isn't the changes that do you in, it's the transitions. Change is not the same as transition. Change is situational: the new site, the new boss, the new team roles, the new policy. Transition is the psychological process people go through to come to terms with the new situation ... Unless transition occurs, change will not work.'

Managing Transitions: Making the Most of Change, William Bridges

This is based on a misapprehension: that change is an objective external. It's a thing, we say, finite and separate from us, just like a customer is separate from us. The customer, we say, is observably either in our database or shop or not. And thus we have believed change to be. Because we believe change to be separate from us, we think we can manage it. But change is not out there, it's everywhere, and in us. (I know that sounds like a tacky Europop song, but it's true). Change is not a box on a chart or a separate module in the MBA, like Strategy; it's the very stuff of business, of life.

By creating this image of change as external, separate, ill-behaved, a thing, the Smart Change Master knows that we only increase our loneliness from it, reduce our identification with it, make it our enemy. Change is not the enemy. In fact, like all living things, we are in a very intimate relationship with change. So intimate in fact that when you begin 'managing change' in an organization you find out very soon that you're simply managing the organization (just better, or differently). And because organizations cannot change except by dint of personal change, you realize that in fact you are managing yourself – how you think, how you act, how you respond to life.

Here's another fallacy: that you manage change. You don't. You simply do not measure or manage change, you measure and manage results, or benefits, or the opportunities that now exist in the world. You manage attitude. You manage activities. You manage emotion. You manage your perceptions. You manage focus. You manage communication. You manage tactics towards a strategy. You manage the way people learn. But you can never, ever manage change. Two words: King Canute.

This book is designed around some positive, smart and people-centered **beliefs** about change (as opposed many change books which have very negative beliefs about change and see people as part of the problem). And it is based around some very simple **principles**.

Here they are:

The beliefs

Everything changes.

Therefore:

- everything can be changed

- there are no change resistors

- there are no change saboteurs

- there are no 'black holes' in organizations where change doesn't penetrate

- there are no disloyal employees

- ... except the ones we have created by our actions in the past

- ... and all things can be changed

- ... so we can change that reality

- we can recreate what we have done

- the only 'problem people' in organizations are those who haven't yet been given the time, information, psychological space, training or, indeed, the choice to change

- ... or us, because we've misunderstood both the simplicity *and* the difficulty of change.

The principles

1. Awareness

- Know what you want

- know where you are.

2. Alignment

- Change your behaviors, your systems and your attitudes until they are in alignment with what you want

- maintain awareness to help track your progress

- work with what works; learn from and discard what doesn't.

These principles are simple – but they are not easy.

Being deadly serious about change

Change is always possible, but it takes what the philosopher Andrew Cohen calls 'deadly seriousness'.

There is a difference between being serious and being deadly serious. When you are deadly serious, you do not have any time to waste, and this makes your relationship with the Truth very different from when you are just serious. When you are serious you have time, but when you are deadly serious you do not have time at all.

People who are deadly serious succeed; people who are not serious do not succeed. If you want to succeed, you have to make sure you do. It's up to you. If you make sure you do, then you will. And if you're deadly serious, nobody and nothing will be able to stop you.

Most organizations are serious about change but not deadly serious. Change is not the most important thing in the world for them, it's probably about third of fourth on the list after *maintaining shareholder value* and *pleasing the customer*. And they produce change results to match.

But if the change principles above are so simple, why aren't they easy too?

Awareness is simple – we've just got to see things as they are and imagine them better than they are. This is not difficult (although many organizations fail at this first hurdle by dismissing vision as unrealistic, being more comfortable with blame than hope).

What *is* difficult in awareness is facing up to the reality of what we have produced in our work (not many organizations are that humble); and then admitting how far from our dreams we are (not many organizations are that honest). The other difficult thing about awareness is that it takes you to a point where you realize that the only reason you are who you are is you. The only reason a company is the way it is is because it has chosen to think and behave the way that it has. It is not how it is because of increasing competition, demanding customers, or advancing technology – the result of tough times. It is how it is because of how it has responded to these things. Taking responsibility for what the company has produced in the past – however painful or embarrassing that might be – is an essential stage in change.

Alignment, too, is simple, and probably gets easier the more you do it. Alignment is about allowing a clear pathway to open up between reality and vision, where everything you have in the organization is pointing towards and helping your vision. This 'everything' includes:

- strategy

- tactics

- attitudes

- budgets

- branding

- marketing

- hiring and firing criteria

- decision-making processes

- systems

- appraisals

- pay and rewards

- leadership behavior

- the decor

- meetings

- the office layout

- training and development

- advertising and marketing

- interaction with outside stakeholders (customers/suppliers/families/ shareholders/community)

- the Christmas party

- the design of the reception area

- payment of creditors

There's a lot that can get in the way of the vision, there's a lot that can be misaligned. It's the difference between:

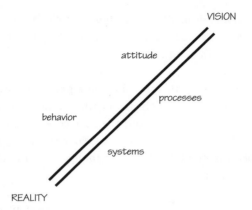

and:

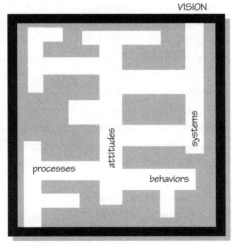

Visions get lost in the maze of misalignment. Mazes can be extremely frustrating places to be, if you're interested in getting somewhere quickly. If you're not, then they are wonderful places for sucking up energy. Mazes can generate a tremendous illusion of busy activity. Sometimes, however, mazes are extremely seductive places to be. People can walk about in them for years, as if in a trance.

The simplicity of these principles does not preclude discipline or even toughness. Organizations which are deadly serious about change will face up to what they find out about themselves – the good, the bad and the humiliating. And, once they have set their vision, they will simply not tolerate deviations from alignment. The change becomes the most important thing in the world to them.

Suppose the vision was part of a corporate commitment toward 'adding value'. If a company is *serious* about that, they publish the vision in a nice document and employ one of the huge consultancies to re-engineer a process or two. If a company is *deadly serious* about it, then every thing that it does, every possible way in which it spends its time, every administration system, every meeting, every appraisal, is held up and examined against that light. The company simply stops spending time on things that don't add value. No excuses. What works ('adding value') is kept. What doesn't work ('not adding value') is thrown out. The difficult thing is that many of the things that have served a company well and to which they have grown attached may now be inappropriate. Those things have to be discarded. That loss can be hard.

Alignment is incredibly hard work. One of the biggest problems change leaders face is watching their organization snap back to the old ways of doing things. After all, those old ways are very comfortable – they took many years of conditioning – so it's natural that people would want to return there. Alignment takes a clear and overt redesign of systems and processes to make that snap back near impossible; it also takes constant attention, concentration, watchfulness, imagination, insistence and per-

We'd just announced a significant loss in the last financial year. 'Difficult trading conditions' had been exacerbated by serious errors of judgment by some of our senior managers. It was rough. So we went away, the board, on a retreat to sort out what we were going to do in the future as a result of these (for this company) unprecedentedly hard times. We took a consultant along as a facilitator. He was very tough on us, which with hindsight I can see was necessary, but at the time it just felt like another the way the world was conspiring against us. First thing he asked us was to talk about our fears – what we were most scared of. 'Failure', we said, unanimously, almost without thinking. Then he asked us to talk about our company's strengths, what we do well, what we were proud of. I remember we came up with a long list, and we stuck the pieces of flip chart paper on to the wall. We all looked at the list of strengths. I did at least. I thought it would inspire me. But the facilitator didn't want us to be inspired just yet. 'We cannot talk about the future', he said, 'until you understand that the combination and interaction of exactly this list of strengths has produced for you what you most fear. Your fear – failure – has happened to you, and this is how you got there. There are only two ways forward now, and you must take them both. You must develop new strengths whilst throwing away your attachment to what you loved; and you must change what you fear. There is no point in fearing failure any more, because it is sitting beside you in this room. You must find better things to be afraid of.'

Director of clothing manufacturer

sistence on the part of the change leader to explain why not reverting is a good idea.

When an organization is aligned, the energy of change passes easily through and about the organization as it moves towards its vision. Misalignment blocks that energy, causing friction, shock, exhaustion and confusion. Lots of activity is produced, but little change happens.

Q: What's so great about Change? What will learning to be a Smart Change Master bring to me and my company?

A: Change used to be only for those companies who were losing money or for those individuals who were seen to be struggling and needed 'bringing into line'. Now technological advances, globalization and smarter customers mean that even the healthiest, most innovative organizations need to be in the change game. But it doesn't have to be about pain. Here are just some of the ...

Benefits for the Smart individual:

- increased job satisfaction (from victim-status to mastery of change)
- prestige (not many are good at leading change)
- enhanced employability/marketability (ditto)
- lessons learnt apply in personal life too (better awareness and balance)
- openness to learning, risk, entrepreneurial ideas (confidence)
- understanding of the basic principles of life in organizations (power)

Benefits for the Smart organization:

- refocusing of corporate purpose, identity and energy on achieving new goals (enhanced confidence)
- shedding old, redundant ways of doing things (increased agility)
- new customers, if you choose, or better relationships with current ones (= more/different money)
- attractiveness to smart individuals (= ultimate source of competitive advantage)
- learning faster/becoming smarter (= next most ultimate source)
- survival (optional)

If you need any more benefits, it's too late for your company.

You need to be deadly serious to change. Every step away from the clear, aligned path to change is a step back into the maze of the old ways of doing things.

1

Burning Down the Old House of Change

Seeking a vision of change appropriate to our times

'We are sometime truly to see our life as positive, not negative; as made up of continuous willing, not of constraints and prohibition.'

Mary Parker Follet

The prime mover

So what do you want to do?

- change yourself (your clothes/skills/competence/attitude)?

- change another (influence someone else's attitude towards you or a concept)?

- change a system or process in your business?

- change a corporate culture?

- change business?

- change the world?

Is this a 'degree of difficulty' list? No. The nature of change is constant throughout: the same principles of awareness and alignment apply at each level.

What else links these six changes? In all cases, there's a creation aspect and a death aspect – something that was there before passes away to be replaced by something different or new.

The other major link is that each subsequent change is dependent on the first. You can't change anything unless you shift too. Even if you are just trying to persuade someone that your argument is right, you're not going to be able to do that unless you change your own style, perhaps, or mindset, or the phrasing of your perspective. You can never be the still centre in a whirling storm. Everything is connected. If things need to change, you'll have to change. And if you can change – positively, consciously, creatively – you can also change your world.

> *Smart things*
> *to say about change*
>
> Organizations don't change:
> people change. Organizations
> change in units of one.

All change in organizations requires personal change. It's the smart bottom line.

Modern organizations have flexible structures and 'flat hierarchies' in order to speed decision-making and communication. But that will be no good unless you feel confident enough to share your knowledge freely and without ego for the general good.

Modern organizations work in teams rather than as isolated individuals, but that will be no good unless *you* know how to get along with others, create synergy of ideas and dissipate conflict.

Modern organizations rely on reacting quickly to information derived from new customer needs, but that will be no good unless *you* are able to let go of old habits and conditioning and take and advocate healthy risks.

Modern organizations rely on continuous improvement in what they do through constant feedback from their main stakeholders. But this will be no good unless *you* have the courage to challenge the status quo.

If everyone is relying on everyone else to do and be these things, then 'the organization' will never get the results it seeks.

So the company needs *you* to have a mastery of personal change. You will also require this mastery to become more effective in your job.

As a leader of others, you'll need to be the change you are advocating, a model for others. Change creates new worlds (new companies, new systems, new behaviors) and because they're new, there won't be any information about them (no brochures in the corporate travel shop). This demands that you'll have to show people (as well as tell them) what you intend.

You'll also need to maintain balance when things get rough. This means being in greater control of your own consciousness and behavior than your colleagues are of theirs. When the situation requires an even perspective, seeing it just like it is, you cannot afford to be a victim of the distorting effects of your own fears and doubts. When the situation requires clear, honest communication to cut through the bullshit that some ageing fool is throwing up just to make his own pre-retirement years entertaining, you'll need to put aside your Ego's exhortation that 'your job is a stake' and speak the truth, from the heart. You'll need to be clever, certainly, in your work as a change leader. But many people can be clever. Not many have the desire to work on themselves so that their thinking is clear and balanced, their emotions flowing without block or agitation and their body free from stress and exhaustion. Cleverness tends to evaporate when you feel like you've been dragged through a hedge backwards over the coals on a roller coaster.

Effective organizational change is rooted in a healthy, realistic perspective on personal change.

There are a hundred books, tapes and courses out there that can help you manage your stress, change the way you feel, your restrictive beliefs, your core values, your ability to listen. I do not wish to reproduce their advice here. What I intend to do is help change your Awareness, by giving you the start of a new vision for change, a change perhaps more suitable for the times than the feared, difficult, pain producing, 'external objective' change I described in the last chapter. It is an unashamedly positive vision but as realistic, I believe, as anyone else's.

Good question. What if change *weren't* such a Big Thing? After all, change is potential. It is growth. Learning your way through change places you at the creative centre of your life rather than being a victim of external circumstance.

> *CHANGE IS A BIG THING FOR INDIVIDUALS BECAUSE:*
>
> - We usually see the need for change to be something that happens outside ourselves. Our boss needs to change – or so-and-so in our team, she'd better buck her socks up. 'This company' had better change too, or else I'm off.
> - Making personal change happen is to step outside of the comfort zone. This, by definition, requires us giving up comfort for discomfort – whether that be in the form of learning new skills or letting go of old assumptions and beliefs. And although we will eventually get used to the new world outside the zone, we will for some length of time have to get used to the discomfort. If you're comfortable, the implication goes, you're not changing.
> - Personal change is not just about piling on new things – new habits, behaviors or beliefs. It is about getting rid of the old ones. That means coming to terms with loss.
> - Loss isn't the only discomfort associated with personal change. If you choose to let go of an old habit or attitude, part of the letting-go requires facing up to them, however discomforting that might be, and examining how they got there in the first place. They were yours, those nasty behaviors, that need to bully, or complain, or be angry. You made them. You can't just buy new habits like a new set of clothes. You have to own up to what you've done, so that you can recognize it if you ever start doing it again. That can be hard. The way to the light, unfortunately, is through the darkness.

Honestly, it is, it does. Just swallow this tablet and see.

'Call me old fashioned, but ... ': A more positive outlook on change

What if we took a drug that made us more positive about change? Go on, no-one's looking. There's only you and me here.

A secure base in life can open people up to what is positive in change/learning, progress, improved lives. Lack of a secure base can plunge people down to the most negative and threatening side of change, producing compulsions, habits, addictions and pain.

Diary of a Change Agent, Tony Page

Now, as the drug takes hold I'm going to suggest a few ideas to you. Just relax.

What if change were an adventure, such that you would actually look forward to it? What if, when things appeared to be staying the same for too long, you'd interpret that as deterioration rather than security? What if you *loved* change?

What would happen?

What if change were not a story about how fate keeps punishing you, but an opportunity to reinvent yourself, right now, to join an ever-spinning, universal, time-immemorial, mystical-and-real, life-death-and-rebirth, non-man-made and entirely natural cycle? Try the following exercise:

If change were an adventure and not a threat I would

Be:

Do:

Our world is spinning, our culture is spinning, no-one knows how its going to turn out, all we need to do is trust the process that change really is, really really is the only constant in life, that something so fundamental to the DNA of Life can't have been designed just to mess up your weekend, and that something good is *always* born out of the death of something old. You're going to be OK. No-one else but you can make you not OK. Nor can change ...

Oh yes, change sometimes appears hard, a bum deal, a not-so-good trip. Then again, change is sometimes so easy that it's like falling off a chair into a bed of roses which is greener on the other side wearing rose-tinted spectacles on Easy Street. Finding a twenty-pound note in the street, finding yourself tapping off with a beautiful person at a party when you weren't even trying, hitting the sales targets half way through the quarter even before your team has wiped the sleep from its eyes – that's not hard is it? When change is that easy, you don't need books like this to help you handle it. No-one goes around then warning how difficult it is to deal with resistance to change, do they?

No.

So it's up to you. You can sit around focusing on that difficulty, or you can take your power back inside you and let good things happen. And when change seems harder than that implies, then you'll need to accept that getting the good things is going to require you to invest a bit more of yourself into it.

When change appears hard, you'll need to learn how to be a good self-motivator, talk well and positively of and to yourself, you'll need to know what inside you always gets you to take that First Step towards change (maybe dreaming it in your head, writing it down in your journal or organizer – 'a goal is a dream with a deadline' (Harvey MacKay) – maybe promising yourself a big treat when you're through, maybe enlisting the support of trusted allies).

And then, when the plans have been made and the dream's been had and it's time to make the change, that's when the fear comes.

Fear is not a bad thing nor is it a good thing, not positive or negative. Fear is part of change. What you do with the fear – that's the key.

You can get paralysed by fear or you can get mobilized by the fear. Either way, you'll never stop feeling fear about something or other. Fear is designed to protect the life of the organism when it's in danger, by motivating said organism to get the hell out of there (or, like Elmer Fudd, to be *very*, *very* quiet). Beyond the physical realm, there are many shades of psychological fear. Fear of the unknown, unsurprisingly, is what really gets people down when change is occurring, and anything that is different from what we know now, by definition, is unknown. Any change, no matter how well planned or envisioned the outcome, is a movement into new experience. And for some, that fear of the unknown is as scary as the unseen monster under the bed. Fear of the unknown has many faces. Maybe fear of failure holds you back. Fear of having someone not like you because of the change? Fear of looking foolish? Fear of commitment? How about fear of success, the fear of actually getting what you want (because what will you do *then* ... ?).

So there'll be no end to the fear popping up. It's what you do with the fear that will make or break your life. And, at some point, you'll feel the fear and you'll do it anyway, because you'll understand in the end that the fear is there to show you something valuable about you and the change involved, and you'll learn from that ...

And then there'll be no time left for procrastination. You've sorted out what you want. You've dealt with the part of you which is trying to stop you getting what you want. You've learnt from the fear. There's nothing else to do. Now you need to take that First Step ...

And see what turns out.

It may be what you anticipated and planned and wished for. And maybe it isn't. Either way, the healthiest response is always acceptance. Andrew Cohen, teacher, says that Enlightenment comes from accepting everything exactly as it is, all the time, not wanting anything to be different. Yikes! Can you imagine? Not wanting anything to be different, ever? But I want the world, and everything and everyone in it, to be just as I want it, all the time. I want my wife and children to live up to my expectations, demands and values. I want them to fit into my definition of happiness (which is easy enough – it's 'whatever makes *me* happy, whenever I say so'). I want my job to be exciting when it's dull and secure when things are scary. I want to own lots of stuff now and pay for it later if at all. I want the movie to start when I get home and not before. I want a chicken-and-mayonnaise sandwich, to go, now. No, I want bacon and avocado. No. Tuna. Cheese.

That's all I want. I'm good at trying to get what I want. I've been trying to get my own way since I was a toddler.

What about you?

Multiply you and me by a few thousand and you can see how organizations can turn into pretty nasty places ...

Not against, with.

If you're not accepting, you're using valuable energy struggling against something real which is denying your personal version of reality. And that's ultimately futile. Now some things can be changed, and there are tools for changing them, as this book makes clear (it also assumes that you're not Enlightened – yet – and therefore still want things to be different than they currently are in your work and life). But many things can't be changed by your will and efforts – other people, for example (unless they want and decide to). Many circumstances, similarly, refuse to conform to your agenda, no matter how much you worry or pout. The energy you throw out trying to change things which are outside your scope of influence will come back to you in the form of anxiety, bitterness, blame, regret and self-pity. Fighting battles you cannot win, tilting against windmills, is the surest way to live your life as a victim. Let go. The trick for the Smart Change Master is knowing what and how to change what you can, and forgetting about – accepting – the rest.

Sounds simple, eh?

Well, it is simple. It is profoundly, ridiculously simple. It's just ...

[Oh, I see that the drug is beginning to wear off now ...]

It's just not *easy*, that's all ...

But whether you got what you wanted or not, you'll eventually look back and see that what you've been through, no matter how small or grand, has given you the chance to learn something about the transcendent values of life, like faith, hope, courage, serenity and wisdom. And if *that* is always the result of change, no matter whether it appears to be materially 'successful' or not – then how can change be a bad thing?

It's not and never has been. Our toddler fear – not getting our own way – that's what may still be a bad thing for you and me.

And then, because you'll have been changed by this experience of moving and learning consciously through change (whether you got what you wanted or not), things will again shift and stir inside you and you'll give birth to the intention to change something else in your world.

And the cycle of change will flow on again.

Awareness

- know what you want

- know where you are.

Alignment

- change your behaviors, your systems and your attitudes until they are in alignment with what you want

- maintain awareness to help track your progress

- work with what works; learn from and discard what doesn't.

Characteristics of two paths of change

Path 1	The Path Less Traveled
Change from outside – take what you can get	Change from inside – create it
Own the product: love the result	Own the process: love the journey
Optimism/pessimism vacillation	Faith & trust in what's happening
Blame others if you don't get what you want	Accept what happens; learn from it
Gratitude if you get what you want (maybe)	Gratitude for all outcomes

[There. I've always thought organizations would be better places with more drugs around.]

Ten things to remember about fear

- Fear is natural and unavoidable – so simply acknowledge it and push on. Mobilize, don't paralyze.

- Remember personal power comes from the inside: believe in yourself.

- Take responsibility for what you do or don't do; avoid blaming others or the world.

- Think positively.

- Leave the tribe – think, decide and act for yourself.

- Make 'no-lose decisions' – those that allow you to learn even from disaster.

- Work in all aspects of your whole life: fear in the work area will impact outside it too.

- Don't resist reality, let go of it – what you resist, persists.

- Give away what you want – if you want trust, trust others; if you want praise, praise others.

- Be gentle on yourself – the world may criticize and mock, but there are more constructive ways that you can deal with negative outcomes.

[adapted from *Feel the Fear and Do It Anyway*, Susan Jeffer.]

That world has so long thrived through bright minds and strong hands doing hard work that it is easy to get drawn into the delusion that pure effort brings successful change. Would that it were that easy.

What are the chances of transferring my vision of change into the rough, tough, 'we never fail' world of organizations?

Well, it starts with you. Following are ten questions to ask yourself about any change you intend working on.

Ten change truths that apply in both the personal and organizational realms

I've drawn this list from my own observations of both successful and unsuccessful change projects. Both sorts were populated by talented and largely well-intentioned individuals. But talent seems not to be enough unless the following simple principles are followed too:

1. You have to decide exactly what it is that you want ... have you?

Unclear goals create unclear outcomes. Following the temptation to leap in and start work without enough thought and planning produces wasted energy and lots of disillusionment. A clear goal directs energy, gives a sense of purpose and provides a context for resolving any problems. See the chapter on Vision-making for further help.

2. You have to really want the change ... do you?

The change is not an option; it *must* happen. There is no alternative, no matter how busy the organization, no matter what might crop up two months from now. If there is an alternative, don't bother starting. Many change projects start life as 'a pretty good idea' that's 'probably worth the effort in the long run; let's get going and see if anything crops up later along the line.' These saintly efforts are easy prey for people who would like to play the role of change assassins lurking on the 3rd floor. Don't let your project take a mugging.

3. You have to own it ... do you?

Someone must make this change happen and take responsibility for everything it produces (whether that's anticipated or manageable or not). Someone has to be clearly identified with the project, not just when its very fashionable and full of hope and the best players, but also when it begins to piss people off and your best players leave to work on something that 'cropped up later along the line'. Someone has to carry the can, because many people in organizations would rather play 'pass the parcel'. Someone has to. Someone has to. Erm – any ideas who?

4. You have to be realistic ... are you?

The change may well be painful and costly for you as much, if not more so, than the people around you. The pain and cost will come, before, during or after the change project, but come it will. Are you resilient enough to take it? Realism also comes through accepting how much work is involved in keeping individuals and organizations aligned with the change vision, when all their instincts are screaming at them to get back to the old way of doing things. Are you strong enough to keep them moving forwards?

5. You have to know what gets in the way of changing ... do you?

Get fascinated by the current habits, practices or behaviors that will resist change. Get to know them intimately. How did they get there, how are they reinforced? What do they give to the people who support them? What's your strategy – attack them head on or ignore them completely (either can be appropriate)? You have to use Darwinian levers: give power to the strong and take power from the weak. In this context, strong means all the positive things you want to achieve. Praise them, reward them, reinforce them, celebrate them, repeat them, repeat them, repeat them, publicize them happening. You have to punish the old behaviors when they happen – and make it very clear why you corrected them.

6. *You have to be positive ... are you?*

Attitude and self-belief are key drivers of change. Don't play the 'but' or 'maybe' game. Doubt slaughters change. Try not to be side-tracked by fear.

7. *You have to be optimistic ... are you?*

Thomas Watson, founder of IBM is attributed with the line: 'if you want to achieve excellence, you can get there today; as of this second, quit doing less than excellent work.' Deciding to make any change takes an instant – sustaining it is the challenge. At the same time, you have to know that the change *can* happen now – it may not have to take a lifetime – because you will lose motivation (and that of those around you) if you decide you will only be satisfied when the final goal has been achieved. Most standard change programs are long and complex. Some are so long that there's a good chance that you won't be around to see it end. Some change destinations change even as the project is in motion. So focus on the journey as well as the destination.

8. *You have to be aware ... are you?*

Raise awareness by asking:

- What's happening to take us towards the goal?

- What's happened last week that failed to move us forward, or took us down old paths that we agreed we wanted to change?

- What specifically can each of us we do next week that will move us towards our goal?

9. You have to let it happen ... do you?

It seems a contradiction to say, as I do, that a clear sense of what you want gives you a motivating direction and purpose and then also say that you should let go of what will happen. Allowing your purpose to unfold as it will is an exhortation to stay flexible. That's why keeping aware of what is happening around you as you walk on the path of alignment is just as important as setting the vision in the first place. The point is that unless you remain detached and flexible, you may miss opportunities for learning how to get to the same goal quicker, smarter, better. And you'll certainly miss the fun. There is every reason to be disciplined, conscientious, 'professional'. There is no reason to become obsessed and rigid.

10. You have to be grateful ... are you?

You have to be grateful for whatever turns up, since even a negative outcome or a piece of resistance teaches you something about how not to get to where you are going. You have to be grateful to others, since change rarely happens in isolation. Through someone else's efforts, ideas or even (in the case of would-be opponents of change) their getting out of the way, you have succeeded. It would be churlish not to be grateful – and probably damaging to your chances of succeeding next time.

> Q: How long will the change take?
> A: When can a person who has quit smoking be said to have changed his behavior? At the moment of decision? After the first day? After the first month, when the worst cravings are said to have subsided because of changing body chemistry? They say an alcoholic is always *recovering* but has never *recovered*, but that doesn't negate the achievement of every day without booze. Does this thinking work in organizational change too?

Smart answers to tough questions

Take the story of Semco. Ricardo Semlar, Brazilian star CEO and author of the book *Maverick*, radically changed the way Semco, his company, operated by implementing some astonishing empowerment practices when most HR Directors in Europe were still fretting over the meaning of the word.

Semlar admitted that he had successfully changed the behavior of his people. They acted in a manner that was more mature, responsible, self-managing, decisive, fast than before his tenure – and this had had extremely positive benefits for the health and performance of his company. Most change programs focus on changed behavior as the only and final proof that the change is real, but Semlar had his doubts about what had happened to his staff's underlying attitudes. He confessed that he thought that they were behaving in the new way really because he'd *told* them to do so (and in effect threatened them with redundancy if they didn't). In that sense, the implication was, he had influenced them to change in exactly the way that any boss who produces negative behaviors does – by forcing them to please him.

'So how long do you think it will take for the underlying attitudes to shift to match the behavior; to get them to behave that way because they want to for themselves?' he was asked.

'Oh, said Semlar, 'I guess about a generation ... '

In other words, change can happen in an instant – and can take an awful long time too.

Now that we understand more clearly what change attitudes and behaviors are most appropriate, it is time to set them in the context of how change is happening in the world.

A brief history of change

Almost every management theory or guiding idea is associated with controlling the rate, direction or impact of change on the organization. Here are five of the key developments in 20th-Century organizational improvement:

Frederick Taylor – Scientific Management (c. 1911f)

Focusing on the design and execution of distinct tasks, optimizing efficiency and productivity; management by theory producing industry-standard (rather than company-specific) production rates.

Max Weber – 'The Classical (Administrative) School' (c. 1920f)

A similarly emotionless approach to performance improvement this time at the level of organization rather than individual task. Focus on military-like, well-run bureaucracy; individual as cog in the machine following orders via a 'chain of command'. Non-stop fun, probably.

Chester Barnard – 'The Human Relations School' (c. 1924f)

Suggesting that organizations were not machines or engines but co-operative entities; emphasized the role and importance of social relationships, impact of hierarchy, solidarity etc. Gave birth to new understanding of workplace psychology, group dynamics, motivation etc. Probably the birthplace of teamworking, empowerment, learning organizations etc.

Deming, Juran et al. – Total Quality Management (c. 1949f)

The first truly customer-focused management theory; zero tolerance for waste; continuous improvement of tools, procedures, product quality, everything; teamwork across the value chain from employee to supplier; perhaps the 'secret' behind the post-war Japanese economic miracle; many efficiency focused approaches developed: Lean Production, Just in Time Manufacturing, Cycle Time Reduction.

Hammer, Champy – Business Process Engineering (c. 1993f)

'... the radical redesign of business processes to achieve dramatic (cp TQM's incremental) improvement in critical measures such as cost, quality, service etc.'; high promise, high risk, high cost, mixed results; change for iconoclasts; many a roughshod downsizing carried out in BPR's name.

2

Changing Organizations in a Changing World

'Today the management of change is no longer the major problem for organizations. It is the management of surprise.'

Marquardt & Reynolds, The Global Learning Organization

A survey of 200 senior managers in the UK found that 40% of them said that they would need to restructure their organizations every six to twelve months; another 41% said that this would have to be done every two to three years. Consultants at the then Coopers & Lybrands stumbled on one company that had 78 change initiatives currently live.

'Managing change' is the harsh and exhausting reality of organizations today. If you take and keep a career in business, you're either going to be asked to lead change, at some level of responsibility or seniority, or you're going to be lying back experiencing it. Either way, you're not going to avoid it.

The world is shifting, from left to right (see boxes). It would seem that the right is undeniably a better place to live and work. Having said that, do we really need TV movies so quickly? Is our impatience for anything old so intense that Sony thought to develop 227 versions of The Walkman since 1992 (an average of one every 3 weeks)? Did the US consumer really need 64 new varieties of spaghetti sauce in 1991 alone?

Only Tom Peters' numbers are undeniable. The other left and right columns denote trends rather than distinct realities, and there is many a company that has as much left-hand column in it as right. Truly this is an age

---

HOW THE WORLD IS CHANGING 1

You must welcome change as the rule but not as your ruler.

Yesterday	**Today**
natural resources defined power	knowledge is power
hierarchy was the model	synergy is the mandate
leaders commanded and controlled	leaders empower and coach
leaders were warriors	leaders are facilitators
leaders demanded respect	leaders encourage self-respect
shareholders came first	customers come first
managers directed	managers delegate
supervisors flourished	supervisors vanish
employees took orders	teams make decisions
seniority signified status	creativity drives progress
production determined availability	quality determines demand
value was extra	value is everything
everyone was a competitor	everyone is a customer
profits earned through expediency	profits are earned with integrity

From *Empires of the Mind*, Denis Waitley

HOW THE WORLD IS CHANGING 2

Forget five-year plans, try fifty-day plans.

Production Strategy (old world)	Innovation Strategy (new world)
maintain delivery and minimize cost	change with minimal pain
suppression of personal identity	recognition of personal identity
compliance, rule keeping	independence, rule breaking
loyalty to firm	loyalty to self
convergent thinking	divergent thinking
indifference to corporate values	commitment to corporate values
low risk, certainty	high risk, faith
retain status quo	change status quo
motivate with physical rewards	motivate with psychological rewards
love the rewards	love the company

From *Managing Continuous Change*, ITMP Wentworth Research Report, 1995

HOW THE WORLD IS CHANGING 3

Nothing significant will change in the organizational sphere unless personal transformation occurs.

Personal Bias:

create a new standard of living	create a new standard for living
self-gratification	self-knowledge
getting	giving
power over	power with
emphasis on family	emphasis on community/environment
acquisitive	inquisitive
image	integrity
success	significance

© Resonate inc., Consulting Firm, Ohio

of the Fast Company, where innovation rules and people are genuinely valued for their talent and potential. And just as truly is it an age of the old toxic cultures. We are in between times. Ours is a both/and environment, not an either/or.

Nevertheless it's worth the Smart Change Master taking a moment to understand what changes are forcing us all out of the left hand column and into a new world.

Smart quotes

Tempora mutantur et nos mutamur in illis.

(Times change, and we change with them.)

Running fast just to stay still: keeping up with the forces for change

Change is constant. It's going on all the time. And it is moving faster. Everything's a rush, everything's a blur. Everyone you know in business is too busy, yes? Everyone wants more time, right? Tough.

What contributes to the stressful and frightening waves of relentless change? Here are some of the current trends which are making your own experience of life and work radically different from that of your parents (and, possibly, your CEO):

- changing political makeup

- large institution break-up

- technology brings instant global connection

- information overload

- super competitiveness, even across international boundaries

- growing free trade amongst nations

- ecological and environmental pressures

- changing social makeup – family roles shifting

- highest possible quality the norm

- corporate decision-making process spread wide

- authority more openly challenged and questioned

- employee expectations far greater

- smarter, more demanding customers

- pace of life faster.

In response to a changing world, companies attempt to adapt:

- mergers and acquisitions

- globalization

- BPR

- TQM

- core competencies

- values and mission statements

- management by objectives

- outsourcing

- downsizing/rightsizing

- benchmarking

- empowerment

- teams

- customer service

- the company crèche.

The popular way of discussing approaches like those listed above is to call them 'management fads'. The suggestion is that they are foisted on long-suffering employees of organizations led by bosses who have been duped by yet another buzzword wielding management consultant.

Call me defensive – I may after all be yet another buzzword-wielding management consultant – but I don't think that organizations are half as powerless as this popular summary suggests. The idea of gormless organizations having their pockets rifled by charlatan advisors is a silly myth, and negates the alternative – and in my view more accurate – reality: that companies, rather than be overwhelmed by the increasing pace of business, demonstrate remorseless energy and optimism in seeking new ways forward. Saying 'it's just another management fad' is an easy get-out, avoiding putting effort into and taking responsibility for the outcome.

Note: a good way to ensure that you do make your change attempt 'just another management fad' is to implement it off the shelf, out of a book or out of the head of your consultant without long and deep introspection about how the change methodology would fit and affect your organization as it is now, with all its strengths and weaknesses, culture and history. Context is all.

The Smart Change Master knows that each of these 'fads' in fact represents an honest attempt to find a better way to compete and survive. Everyone has perfect vision with hindsight, and every experiment increases our ability to learn from the last idea and implement the next one better. Far from being the idle experiments of decadent and power-crazed leaders, each new theory reminds us that there is little choice in the modern hyper-competitive world but to try something, once more, with feeling. The only other real choice is oblivion. Standing still is deadly.

In the old days of business, clever founders would make whatever decisions were necessary and organize largely tame and dumb employees to carry out the necessary tasks efficiently. The modern business environment is as far from that as is possible to get, and organizations must strive, continually, to:

- accelerate the development of product and process innovation

- anticipate and adapt to environmental changes

- become more proficient at learning from competitors and collaborators

- get closer to the consumer to satisfy customer desires and accumulate market information

- expedite the transfer of knowledge throughout the organization

- learn more effectively from their mistakes

- make greater use of employees at all levels

- shorten the time required to implement strategic decisions

- stimulate continuous improvement in all areas of the company.

(List adapted from *The Global Learning Organization*)

So that is what organizations are trying to do in response to a changing environment. But how does change occur in organizations?

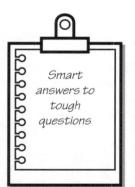

Smart answers to tough questions

Q: Oh no! Not another Big Idea that's going to line the consultants' pockets ...?

A: I'd like to hear from you your summary of the weaknesses of this plan. We're all fallible – and if we've missed anything, we'd be glad to hear your feedback. We've taken a mature decision that outside help will keep us on track for this change and diminish our chances of making unnecessary mistakes. Change is hard – it's always a good idea to have an ally, even if you have to pay for one. Again, if you can tell me how we can reap those same benefits on our own, I'd be happy to listen.

On the complexity of organizational change: four prevalent change models

Andrew Van de Ven of the University of Minnesota, and Marshall Poole from the University of Wisconsin undertook an extensive, interdisciplinary literature review to uncover the many concepts, metaphors and theories used to explain change. They found four basic underlying models* upon which the widespread theories of organizational change appear to be built:

1. The goal-setting model

The organization sets a desired outcome and mobilizes resources to reach it. This is the most common change model in business.

2. The life-cycle model

This reflects the sequential pattern of birth, growth, maturity, decline and death which occurs in all living things. Change happens during each stage of course, but is often most marked in the transition from one stage to another. That's why humans make such a thing of celebrating 'rites of passage' at birth; puberty; adulthood; retirement and burial.

3. The competing forces model

The third model assumes a world in which events, forces and values conflict with each other for dominance. Change or stability is the result of the power struggle between the opposing entities. It is a model which demonstrates all the messy struggles, negotiations and compromises that organizations have every day.

4. The biological evolution model

Here, change occurs in a continuous cycle of variation, selection and retention. Variation occurs naturally and randomly. Selection is determined by competition for scarce resources and environmental fit. Retention is achieved by forces (including inertia) that maintain and perpetuate existing forms. Periods of gradual evolution may suddenly be punctuated by moments of dramatic change.

[*Summaries adapted from *Managing Change*, The Antidote, Issue 14, CSBS]

Poole and de Ven suggest that the chief danger is assuming that only one model is right. More likely, you can probably recognize all four types of change occurring in your organization at once.

Let's have a closer look at them again.

Model 1: *change as a target*

Organizations, traditionally comfortable with a task-orientation, favor the first model, and certainly there is much that can be done to create change and ensure that you are applying discipline, intelligence, skill and momentum to what you do. The idea is that an organization is like a machine, logical, physical, structured and driven by a leader at the top. It's a project management world: set your deliverables, assess your risks, manage your resources with relentless efficiency down the project time lines. Though the primacy of this model is gradually being questioned by the other three, it is still the one you are most likely to participate in most traditional organizations.

Model 2: *change as a cycle*

Poole and de Ven's second model reminds us that things do not always occur in a linear fashion as the first model implies. Moreover, if organizations are made up of people, then surely they must have more living qualities than that of a rational machine?

The second model attempts to redress the balance. Change occurs in cycles as well as straight lines, and not all in sequence. Indeed, *everything* occurs in life-cycles: departments, guiding mind sets, political power. People in your organization are going to be at different stages of the cycle. They'll be participating in competing projects which are at different stages: one person alone could be at the birth stage in one of their projects, the maturity of another and overseeing the dying days of another. Since different styles, attitudes and energies are required at each stage, you can understand why people complain of 'change fatigue'. Change fatigue does not come about just because of the quantity of changes a company attempts, but because of the complexities and prevalence of change in all aspects of the organization's work.

At an individual level, people are often at different stages of their own cycle. Some of your colleagues are approaching the end of their career, others just starting. Some will be facing challenges of identity and self-esteem outside of their work which is going to impact their behavior in it. Communication must treat everyone as an individual.

Charles Handy draws his own version of the change cycle with his Sigmoid Curve, which tells the simple story of rise and fall, wax and wane. Everything travels along the Sigmoid Curve – empires, products, relationships – and they seem to be doing so with increasing speed.

The right place to start that second curve is at point A, where there is the time, as well as the resources and the energy, to get the new curve through its initial explorations and floundering before the first curve begins to dip downwards. That would seem obvious; were it not for the fact that at point A all the messages coming through to the individual or institution are that everything is going fine, that it would be folly to change when the current recipes are working so well. All that we know of change, be it personal change or change in organizations, tells us that the real energy for change only comes when you are looking disaster in the face, at point B on the first curve. At this point, however, it is going to require a mighty effort to drag oneself up to where, by now, one should be on the second curve. To make it worse, the current leaders are now discredited because they are seen to have led the organization down the hill ... A good life is probably a succession of second curves ...

from *The Empty Raincoat*

The secret, says Handy, is to start a new Sigmoid Curve before the first one peters out.

Poole and de Ven's cycles model and Handy's Sigmoid Curve call us to consider what happens when two or more cycles (or curves) overlap. Five implications:

- Without a sense that everyone is operating for the greater good of all and for the organization as a whole, the cycles may cause conflict and competition.

- Those who lead the first cycle need to keep it going long enough to support the efforts of those who are just launched on the new curve.

- They need to do this even though they are managing decline and may be fostering their own demise.

- Those who lead the first cycle will probably not be those who lead the second. (A new broom ...)

- The overlap of cycles can be a time of confusion, since the old may seem to contradict the new and vice versa. It is a time for both/and, rather than either/or, thinking. 'We need the legacy system and we need the new programs.' It is a time for level-headedness and sound judgment, especially when people may be clamoring for the new and fashionable second curve, to the neglect and detriment of the first.

Model 3: change as organic system in stable equilibrium

The image of a company as an organic system is taken a step further with Poole and de Ven's third model. Here the system always tends towards equilibrium, driven by the need to adapt to its changing environment.

Change occurs either through constant improvement or because the organization realizes that it is out of balance with the outside world and swiftly creates a new structure with its own equilibrium.

The consulting firm McKinsey produced the most famous image of such a system with its 7-S model, which depicts a pattern of seven circles – the seven main attributes of an organization: structure, systems, style, staff, skills, strategy and super ordinate goals – held in balance by a web of interconnecting forces and tendencies.

The strongest implications of the organic system model are:

SMART PEOPLE
TO HAVE ON
YOUR SIDE:

RICHARD
PASCALE

'If it ain't broke, break it.'

Richard Pascale made his name as one of the team of four consultants and academics who developed the 7-S framework – strategy, structure, skills, staff, shared values, systems and style – which any company is alleged to hold in equal consideration. Pascale's interest in the Japanese 'economic miracle' of the post-war years led him to suggest that the Japanese success was based on their respect for and investment in the 'soft Ss' – skills, staff, shared values and style – whereas the West concentrated heavily on the 'hard Ss' – strategy, structure, systems. Pascale later advocated the Japanese ideal of vision as a living, energizing action oriented raison d'être – e.g. Kamatsu's *Encircle Caterpillar* – as opposed to the bland generalizations which typify Western efforts at vision.

Pascale's latest work has been into corporate transformation, which requires the involvement and commitment of everyone in the organization. Traditional change programs, says Pascale, are limited by the small number of people who are actually driving them.

- that the times of relative equilibrium should be the times of most learning, reselection, process improvement and capability development. In this way, the organization can be best prepared for the next period of cataclysmic upheaval

- that the tendency towards equilibrium may also be a tendency towards complacency, inertia and 'market-blindness'.

Model 4: *change as biological development*

This model incorporates the latest understanding concerning quantum physics, the new biology, and chaos theory. Margaret Wheatley and Myron Kellner-Rogers in *A Simpler Way* (Berrett-Koehler 1996) paint a captivating image of this strange, creative and unpredictable world. They propose that the process of life is logical – the 'logic of play.'

If the first model – company as machine pumping out results, a still centre in a haphazard world – could be considered the most static image of the organization, Wheatley and Kellner-Rogers' image is by far the most dynamic and vibrant of them all. Rather than the old paradigm of trying to get along despite changes happening to them, this world sees the organization as inseparable from its constantly shifting environment.

It is enough to scare the pants off any self-respecting and control-oriented project manager.

Some ways to take advantage of this new scientific understanding about the ever-surprising and creative aspects of life in relation to organizations can be found in Chapters 10 and 11, which are about sustaining change in learning and making change fun.

Wheatley & Kellner-Rogers propose seven key elements in life's logic of play:

- *Everything is in a constant process of discovery and creating.* Everything is changing all the time: individuals, systems, environments, the rules, the processes of evolution. Even change changes. Every organism reinterprets the rules, creates exceptions for itself, creates new rules.
- *Life uses messes to get to well-ordered solutions.* Life doesn't seem to share our desires for efficiency or neatness. It uses redundancy, fuzziness, dense webs of relationships, and unending trials and errors to find what works.
- *Life is intent on finding what works, not what's 'right'.* It is the ability to keep finding solutions that is important; any one solution is temporary. There are no permanently right answers. The capacity to keep changing, to find what works now, is what keeps any organism alive.
- *Life creates more possibilities as it engages with opportunities.* There are no 'windows of opportunity', narrow openings in the fabric of space-time that soon disappear forever. Possibilities beget more possibilities; they are infinite.
- *Life is attracted to order.* It experiments until it discovers how to form a system that can support diverse members. Individuals search out a wide range of possible relationships to discover whether they can organize into a life-sustaining system. These explorations continue until a system is discovered. This system then provides stability for its members, so that individuals are less buffeted by change.
- *Life organizes around identity.* Every living thing acts to develop and preserve itself. Identity is the filter that every organism or system uses to make sense of the world. New information, new relationships, changing environments – all are interpreted through a sense of self. This tendency is so strong that it creates a seeming paradox. An organism will change to maintain its identity.
- *Everything participates in the creation and evolution of its neighbors.* There are no unaffected outsiders. No one system dictates conditions to another. All participate together in creating the conditions of their interdependence.

Margaret Wheatley & Myron Kellner-Rogers, *A Simpler Way*

Deep structure, deep change

All four change models ask a question: what exactly are we changing?

One of the great breakthroughs in organizational thinking is to begin to understand the role of corporate culture and 'deep structure' in breaking or making change.

Both ideas suggest that what we see of organizations – the way they operate, the behaviors, the interactions, the styles, the processes and systems, the objectives and measures – all of these are in fact the most easily shifted aspects in any change program. What lies 'beneath the surface' – i.e. the values, assumptions and beliefs that inform and influence those visible signs – is more difficult to change.

Behavior, for example, is a surface thing. It can be performed. I can force you to change your behavior when I hold a gun to your head, but I shouldn't be surprised if you revert to your old behaviors when I take the gun away. If I really want the change to stick, I need to get at your values, beliefs and assumptions, since these are the things that inform and control your behaviors – not the other way round. And I will need more than a gun to change those, since you will have been developing and testing them since the hours of your first consciousness. They will be deeply ingrained. They will be hard to shift – even if you too wanted to change them.

In the same way, organizations have found that creating change at the surface level with various carrot and stick motivators only leads to temporary and shallow results.

Incremental change in stable times requires only a gradual adaptation of corporate behavior and processes. Constant improvement is sufficient – and that is a very rational process. The present business environment is presenting challenges so huge that they affect the very nature and purpose of some organizations. This requires 'deep change' – change below the surface at the level of beliefs and values. This is not rational, but stimulates powerful emotions – fear, loss, abandonment, surrender – many of which actually persuade the individual or institution that the status quo is 'better'.

The core beliefs that drive organizations often reside in no one person or persons. Rather they describe the essential truth on which

SMART VOICES

We thought we were so cool and modern. But I realize now that we were being incredibly arrogant. And that wasn't just a surface, behavior thing – you know, clever people behaving obnoxiously. It was down in the underlying beliefs of the company. We had a policy never to talk to pressure groups. We just blocked them out of the equation. We laid down the same service contract before all our suppliers, and demanded obedience. Now I see that these were just manifestations of a core belief that said 'when we control, we win.' Even the fact that we were proud to employ people 'for life' I see now as an expression, however benign, of our desire to master the world. If we had people for life, we could control them for life. It was like we were trying to design in predictability.

Ex Head of Marketing, international oil company

it bases all its interactions with the outside world e.g. *success comes through control*; *success comes through power*. These core beliefs are found subtly reflected in all aspects of an organization, even those that appear positive.

Of course, you'd never find those beliefs advertised in the corporate brochure, not just because they aren't very customer-friendly, but because it requires a superior level of awareness and intensive work to surface core beliefs (and most organizations don't bother). Nevertheless, these core beliefs are there, long outliving their usefulness. 'Success through control' is hardly an appropriate core belief in the world of the right hand columns of page 23 – whose core belief might be summarized as 'success through relationship' or 'success through interdependence'.

Change is fundamentally difficult in organizations because fundamentally, organizations have been created to organize, to systemize, to control inputs and outputs, to reduce unwanted possibilities. The world is no longer like that – and life never was, say Wheatley and Kellner-Rogers – and organizations do not fare well if they have these old core beliefs about control and power. Yet have it they do, because deep structure takes a long time to shift. Many long-established businesses hold core beliefs which served them well in a more stable world. Like people, they find it difficult to let go of the past, particularly if it was a happy and comfortable one and produced satisfactory results.

Change will become easier when and if organizations are created to liberate, to empower, to maximize hoped-for possibilities.

In the meantime, the Smart Change Master has to become comfortable operating at all levels of change.

How deep could a change be?
Changing the purpose of the company

'The only sacred cow in an organization should be its basic philosophy of doing business ... its beliefs.'

Thomas Watson Jr

Actually that is no longer correct. (Then again, who was it who said, sacred cows make the tastiest burgers?). Every 'undiscussable' in a company must be faced – whether it's the Finance Director's bullying behavior, the habit of the CEO to duck confrontation, or the very purpose of the company. (By the way, the former may well be harder to confront than the latter; skilled outside help is probably necessary to discuss undiscussables such as personal style.)

These are the times in which many organizations are being asked to change everything. They are changing their processes and systems to the demands of new technology and elaborated customer needs, but that was always so. Companies are changing their product lines – M&S hasn't *always* been a financial service provider, you know, they used to just sell knickers. From the most reactive change in an organization's meeting practice to the most transformational change of its purpose and principles, companies *are* changing their beliefs.

In fact every company, as soon as it comes into being and imposes itself on the world, expresses at least six sets of belief. Just by doing what it does, it takes a stance on all of the following continuums:

- a belief about the nature of business – is it about shareholder profit or social influence?

- a belief about the nature of truth – is truth is imposed by corporate leaders or discovered through the actions of all?

- a belief about the worth of human beings – should they be exploited or invested in?

- a belief about the potential of human beings – do they need to be forced to work or can they express themselves fully in it?

- a belief about the nature of work – is it about completing tasks – the *what* – or helping the organization to learn better – the *how* and *why*?

- a belief about the nature of human creativity and influence – does it need to be controlled or released?

Many organizations, particularly larger ones, are facing the reality that changing fundamental beliefs of this kind is the only constructive option left. Many large organizations rose to power in a more stable environment using the twin levers of financial might and the intellectual cleverness of a few leaders. In these organizations, people were just the basic units of the economy, truly human *resources*. These same companies are now learning the lesson that only through respecting their people and driving information and power out to even the lowliest staff member, will enough commitment, flexibility and team synergy be released to keep the company alive.

IBM changed from being an arrogant old dinosaur, living its own myth of invincibility, to bright, fast, customer-friendly service organization. To do that, it changed its systems, of course, but ultimately it had to change its own beliefs about what IBM was and had to be.

Beliefs *can* change. Often they *must*.

Linking the four models

For the moment, let's try to balance an examination of the most common change model – the goal-oriented one – with an attempt to open it up to a continuously changing, messy and decidedly non-linear environment.

This can be done by raising the organization's awareness of what it wants to be and what it is; by using communication tools which emphasize meaning rather than message; by empathizing with the fear and doubt that change can invoke in some individuals, and by maximizing creativity, enjoyment and learning.

How to do this is the subject of the remainder of this book.

3

The Change Process

'The future is made in the present.'

Kelly Andrews, US Labor Department

Making change happen in organizations requires two major components. Firstly, an overarching methodology or approach maps out all the stages of the change process and creates a picture of what activities and tasks will need to be carried out into the future. Secondly, a set of tools and interventions takes the methodology off the page and makes the change happen in real time.

Traditional approaches to goal-oriented organizational change

Almost all change methodologies share the following characteristics:

1. They seek an improvement to key performance factors of the organization.

2. They seek to make changes in all aspects of the organizational system (that organizations are systems means that it is not possible to make a change in one area without affecting another variable elsewhere).

3. Transformational changes are those that change leadership style, culture, strategy, corporate purpose etc. Transactional changes are those that bring about changes in management practices, systems, processes etc. (Changes to the latter are generally considered easier – and quicker – than changes to the former; it is also generally accepted that changes in the latter will eventually fail or falter without change in the former to underpin them.)

4. They follow a process and therefore sequence for introducing change. Generally this means some sort of:

   - *vision stage:* creating a picture of what things could look like in an ideal world; this gives birth to a change strategy

   - *analysis stage:* gathering data on how things currently are

   - *redesign stage:* planning the tactics and refiguring the processes and systems

   - *implementation stage:* puts the strategy and plans into practice through introducing the new ways of working, retraining, re-education, etc.

   - *review stage:* an attempt both to measure success of the project and to seek new ways of pushing the organization into a new change.

The change process as a cycle, underlining the never-ending journey that change involves. Although there is a goal – implied by shared benefits and measures – in reality the goal is never reached, because the learning and transformation that the organization goes through naturally provides new goals in the process.

Changing in the light

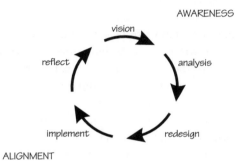

Note that this does not say:

Changing in the dark

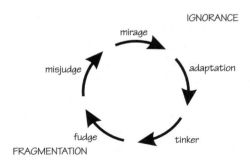

although it is the constant challenge of the smart change leader to prove that theirs is the light cycle. Furthermore each stage of the dark side cycle is a potential pitfall that any change program may fall into.

But where and how does change begin?

Beginning to change

If something which is constant can be said to have a start, change doesn't really begin with the vision or with the strategy or with the analysis. It doesn't even begin with the leadership. It starts beyond the company, outside in the real world, nay, out in the universe, where spinning planets sometimes are in the ascendant, and sometimes not, and thus they effect the humor of your neighbors, the ebb and flow of the tides and the rise and fall of the stock markets. Somewhere an organization has to react. In Iowa, perhaps Mars is in Uranus, and an offensively odored but immensely talented ex-student writes a certain combination of code which seals his fortune and threatens to condemn the mediocre efforts of the established software houses to history – unless they react. A complex intermingling of industrial innovation, half-hearted economic experimentation, overthrows of government, cultural education, cable TV and personal greed causes people to be more demanding about the sort of car they drive. Somewhere, a company has to stop doing things the way they were. They certainly have to stop designing and making cars like they used to. They also have to stop thinking about cars like they did. They have to refigure their conception of customer care, of customers even. They have to move a long-established and recalcitrant organizational system from the manufacturing industry into the service industry. This is where change begins. It's my little theory on *The Astrological Influence of Organizational Change*, a slim companion volume to the present one.

The context is all. Keeping an eye on the context is key.

The mediaeval king listened to the guy on the in the lookout tower who could tell him if any enemy troops were making a move on the castle. And he also listened to the sooth-sayer, who told him what future the crystal ball and horny toad indicated might be coming. The mediaeval King was well covered when it came to assessing the environment.

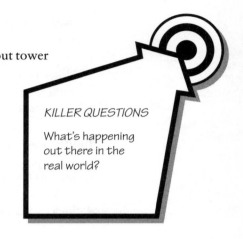

KILLER QUESTIONS

What's happening out there in the real world?

One of the critical success factors of any organization should be the means it has for hooking into the outer realms, its ways of imbibing information from an ever-changing world. How well it does that – how clear it keeps its channels open – can be critical.

All changes initiated in organizations are reactive. None are proactive. Organizations react to changing consumer demands, to the actions of competitors. They are driven by fear (that there won't be enough customers in the future) or envy (that someone might be doing it better elsewhere). Even those that initiate true innovation are reacting to a moral or intuitive imperative in the leader.

So what could cause you to instigate a change?

- What are we listening for at the moment?
- How well are we tuned into the world outside our organization?
- If we had a watchman, where would we ask him to look?
- If we had a fortune-teller, what questions about the future would we ask her?

KILLER QUESTIONS

- the desire to build on a massive, unprecedented and so far unique success

- dissatisfaction with customer service levels

- dissatisfaction with productivity

- dissatisfaction with morale

- dissatisfaction with communication

- the loss of key staff

- the hiring of a maverick

- a brilliant idea for a better way

- a new technology on the market

- the actions of a competitor

- a new government regulation

- a general sense that things should be re-energized

- in order to find a shared purpose that makes your difference from your competitors apparent.

Good questions which drive each stage

The activities that need to be carried out to take an organization around the light cycle of change are implied by a set of questions. Why? Because change, although it can be guided by a model such as this one, can never be prescribed. There has never been an organization like yours ever. There is no organization like yours now, nor will there be. Yours is a unique organization, and you must find out your own answers, your own solutions.

The vision stage

- What would this organization look/sound/feel like if the change had occurred successfully?

- What differences would we expect to see in our major stakeholder areas – customer, community, employee, performance in the market?

- Is this vision in alignment with our overall business strategy and if not, how we will we manage the necessary transformation and expansion?

- How much do we want that – do we want it above everything else?

- What actually needs to change to achieve it – behavior? attitude? internal bureaucracy?

- What are the main goals that this Vision suggests?

- What plans do we need to manage these goals?

- What deadlines and other 'signposts' can we put in place to demonstrate to all that the change is working?

- How will we be able to shift the organizational culture so that the changes don't regress to previous standards or behaviors?

- Who will lead and facilitate this change at the top, and what will be his or her network of change influencers?

- How realistic/stretching/understandable/motivating is this Vision?

- What are the major priorities and preoccupations currently that might get in the way of the change process?

- Can we afford it?

The analysis stage

- How does this organization tend to think/feel/talk/behave?

- How does this organization talk about change?

- What is the capacity of this organization for change?

- How have previous initiatives fared in this company? What happened?

- What barriers to change exist here?

- Where does power lie?

- What is the decision-making process?

- How flexible or adaptable are we? How quickly do things move around here?

- What is the state of communication here?

- What is the degree of change necessary – whole company transformation of beliefs? single group system of process?

- What will be the likely impact of this change on the company?

- What are our strengths and weaknesses?

- How open is conflict?

- How does this company handle a shock to the status quo?

The redesign stage

- Who needs to be in the change team?

- What levers might we use to change things – structure? systems? pay and remuneration? education?

- Which processes/systems need to be redesigned to meet the change requirements?

- What new structure, job roles, job specifications or personnel are required?

- What will be the rewards, checks and measures that encourage the new behaviors?

- What else will we do to shift attitude and change behavior?

- What level and type of outside help do we need?

- What communication channels, strategies and tactics are open to us?

- How will we manage other stakeholders – customers and suppliers, for example, whilst this change is moving?

- Where does power need to reside to ensure change happens?

- What performance measurement systems or information feedback loops will we need to ascertain that we're on track?

- What new or adapted skills and knowledge will we have to make provisions for?

- Will it be possible to run a test of the redesigned process before rolling it out to the whole organization?

The implementation stage

- Are the new education and training needs that this change requires being addressed?

- Is the power base shifting in the required way?

- How excited do people appear to be about the changes?

- How able do they feel in their new roles/jobs/positions/behaviors?

- What skill enhancement is still needed? What attitude shift is still needed?

- What information/action will maintain momentum?

- How are the changes being institutionalized in the systems and processes of the company?

The review stage

- Are the change plan deadlines and signposts being met?

- Are attitudes and behaviors shifting?

- Are our change sponsors still committed?

- What are our continuing budget and resource needs?

- What are we learning that we should use to reinvigorate this change effort?

- How are we recording our learning so that future generations in this company know what happened?

- What opportunities are arising for other change work in the company?

Q: What does Vision mean? Or Purpose? How do Values fit in?
A: These things mean whatever we agree that they'll mean. No-one has ever set these in the stone, so we're not breaking any rules if we play around with them. So again, what *do* we *want* these terms to mean? How about this as a starter glossary?

Vision	a vivid picture of what it will look like when we arrive in the future
Strategy	the long-term decisions and direction that will shape its path to the future
Mission	a clear and compelling business goal
Values	the core, unshakable beliefs we have about what's important to us
Purpose	the answer to the question 'why are we here?'
Goals	shorter-term milestones that we will pass on the way to the Vision

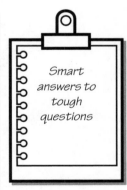

Smart answers to tough questions

'Every organization has a destiny: a deep purpose that expresses the organization's reason for existence. We may never fully know that purpose, just as an individual never fully knows her individual purpose in life. But choosing to continually listen for that sense of emerging purpose is a critical choice that shifts an individual or a community from a reactive to a creative orientation.'

From *The Fifth Discipline Handbook*, Peter Senge *et al.*

Seven plans you'll need to have up your sleeve in any change program

'Make no little plans; they have no magic to stir men's blood.'

Daniel Hudson Burnham

- A plan to ascertain the specific roles and responsibilities (if in doubt, see Chapter 9)

- a plan for influencing the role players to participate (if in doubt, see Chapter 5)

- a plan for ensuring that those who are affected by the change are not just willing but able to change with it (if in doubt, see Chapter 6)

- a plan for learning from what is happening, in order to truly determine 'success' (if in doubt, see Chapter 10)

- a plan for setting and measuring results (if in doubt, see Chapter 8)

- a plan for dealing with failure and success (if in doubt, see Chapter 12)

- a plan for how to stop planning and start doing (if in doubt, see Chapter 1).

Top-down vs bottom-up change

One of the chief assumptions behind change management methodologies is that organizational change is 'top-down'.

Most change is seen as being championed by the vision and passion of the leader. Charismatic, heroic leaders who by force of will and character overcome all obstacles are in fact few and far between. The literature gives the same old suspects: Virgin's Richard Branson, Chrysler's Lee Iacocca, Wal-Mart's Sam Walton. In ten years in business, I've met one leader who I would put into the charismatic category, and heard stories about a friend's experience of one other. The majority of us get by as best we can.

The positive thing to bring out of this reality is that every tool or technique in this book can effectively be used by anyone. And none of them depend on you having to wear a big S on your T-shirt. Unless you want to.

On the other hand, it's difficult to imagine a major organizational change literally being led from the 'bottom', without the direction and sanction of top leadership (picture bands of disgruntled employees bearing flaming torches and farm hand tools, storming the Director's Dining Room). In the change literature, 'bottom-up' actually denotes a more inclusive and democratic approach, rather than a revolutionary one.

How do I choose between the two approaches?

The key factor in deciding how relevant such bottom-up democracy is to your change program is how many potential resistors there are. If your

A German-born psychologist, Kurt Lewin has heavily influenced the whole field of organizational change. He founded a research centre for group dynamics at MIT in 1944.

His most influential piece of research suggested that democratic groups work more effectively than those led by command and control, which is no massive insight now, but in an era dominated by corporate dictatorship and scientific management, his work was ground-breaking. The implication of this is that since a manager is not like a king forcing his will on others, he needs to be an amateur yet accomplished psychologist, understanding what people need and how they operate, in order to influence them effectively.

Two ideas in particular set Lewin apart as a major contributor. The first is the concept of force fields. Here fields of opposing forces hold groups processes in a state of equilibrium. 'Driving forces' such as ambition, goals, needs and fears either move the group away from something they do not value, or towards something they do. 'Restraining forces' conversely, oppose the driving forces – they might be characterized as apathy or group inertia. The two forces cancel each other out when they are equal and this is when a group achieves equilibrium.

In order to create change, then, we must strengthen the driving forces towards a better goal. Take an example with a specific objective. Introducing financial incentives to increase a team's conversion of sales is one alternative (threatening the sack is another). Removing the 'restraining forces' in this example could be achieved by training the team in better closing techniques or in some other way decreasing the difficulty of the objective. Companies have been traditionally more comfortable with the easy option: if you want people to behave well, pay them a bit more. The trouble with this knee jerk reaction, Lewin suggests, is that it may have a short-term benefit, but paying people more does nothing towards reducing the stress associated with carrying out difficult tasks. This stress may have damaging long-term effects, and may also bind the team against the company. Individuals earn more, stress levels increase, morale plummets. It is a costly and unattractive option for the company even though it seems the easiest up front.

In this way, Lewin was one of the first to suggest that managing people was not about controlling them but about taking the time, and showing the care, to invest in their needs. More particularly is the idea that 'resistance to change' might need not necessarily be a behavioral decision by a wilfully obtuse worker, but may be present in the conditions of his or her job.

Lewin's second major contribution is the concept of a three-part process in change unfreezing the current state, moving it, then freezing it in a new place. Whilst this was seized on as a logical and linear process of managing change, in fact Lewin again takes us into the complex and shifting world of group dynamics – and indeed into the same concepts that inform theories concerning corporate culture. He points to the shared norms, values and behaviors that any group establishes as being something that eventually becomes so habitual and comfortable that the group resists it against any significant change. The routines and patterns of group behavior become a positive bond, and can only be lowered in one of two ways. The first way is by reducing the value of something which the group previously held as important. The second is by fundamentally changing what the groups values. Doing this, like most of what is commonly known as soft stuff, is hard work, but here Lewin returns to his democratic research. He finds that well-informed group discussions, at which the group itself decides to take on new values and behaviors is far more effective than a one-to-one coercive presentation by an outsider. Providing the information, creativity and safe space that a group needs to do this would be the sign of a smart change agent in action.

company employs a large majority of stick-in-the-mud, die-hard traditionalists who moan on about the good days, and tell you at every opportunity three new reasons why your change *won't* work, then don't waste too much time trying to enrol them (although *waste enough to see if you can be proved wrong*). This is business, not a love-in. Your option here is to use the prime elements of top down approaches – political power and force.

It is tempting to impose our goals on other people, particularly our children and subordinates. It is tempting for society to try to impose its priorities on everybody. The strategy will, however, be self-defeating if our goals, or society's goals, do not fit with the goals of others. We may get our way but we don't get their learning. They may have to comply but they will not change. We have pushed out their goals with ours and stolen their purposes. It is a pernicious form of theft which kills the will to learn.

from *The Age of Unreason*, Charles Handy.

If, on the other hand, you're surrounded by young turks champing at the bit, then give them their head (almost). The best change is self-driven, and the more you can allow people to learn to own the change, the more effective, resilient and lasting the change will be. In this case, drive the setting of the smaller goals that will, added together, take the organization towards its Vision out to 'the bottom'. Let the 'the bottom' review progress. Let 'the bottom' feed back information. Let 'the bottom' have every opportunity to influence the decisions you're making on what could happen next.

COMPARE AND CONTRAST (A)

A classic top-down approach

1. establish a sense of urgency
2. create the guiding coalition
3. develop a vision and strategy
4. communicate the vision
5. remove obstacles to the new vision
6. generate short term successes
7. consolidate gains and produce more change
8. anchor new approaches in the corporate culture.
   from *Leading Change*, John Kotter, HBS Press 1996

A classic inclusion, top- and bottom-driven approach

Valerie Stewart in *The David Solution* offers a different perspective on the top-down / bottom-up debate. Describing 'middle management' as 'resistant to change', she supposes that they would therefore be a significant barrier to attempts of top management to filter their change strategy down and through the organization. Her idea is that top management take their strategy direct to the pivotal jobs: the junior managers and senior supervisors 'the people from whom you receive the most impact on customer perception per square foot of person employed.' There they gain understanding and commitment and enrol and empower the work force. As the 'bottom' begins to implement the change, the 'middle' is in effect squeezed by the pressure and exhortations of the top and the fact that reality is already changing underneath them. Moreover, by communicating directly to the junior staff, the leaders motivate those crucial people who still have the years and the energy to give to the company. In this way, they ensure that the next generation of middle managers are more proactive than the current one.

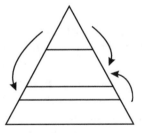

All change: merging top- and bottom-driven approaches

Certainly, in this era of flatter organizations, the terms top and bottom are less relevant than they were. Since many organizations seek to push out the power to those at the periphery – those nearest the customers and the marketplace – it follows that these people will also be closest to shifting customer demands or marketplace transitions that necessitate a change in corporate approach. In this sense, those that bring this critical information could be thought of as a source of change. But geeing people up by telling them that 'this change depends on you' is always going to draw cynicism, because it's not true. It doesn't depend on anybody, it depends on everybody. In truth, we all play a part in another cycle of interdependence: 'workers' generate information and feedback; 'bosses' interpret it and set direction; 'workers' and 'bosses' manifest the direction. No change can work without both sides demonstrating commitment through effective action. A weak link in one part of the system affects the health of the whole system. The trouble is, so much of our thinking to do with work and organizations are based on hierarchical and political beliefs. One of the results of this is that in times of stress the workers always blame the bosses and the bosses blame the workers. In all my years of carrying out climate surveys and cultural audits, I never heard anybody say: 'It's my fault.'

Educating people to get beyond their limiting beliefs about where power lies and who's 'really responsible' for change is a major task in your change leadership. One of your greatest challenges will be getting people on side. Part of this involves getting them to accept that their work is important, to see how it connects with the work of others and the whole organization; that both the work and the connection to the whole system are worthy of ownership by them and therefore worthy of constant improvement.

Whichever approach you take in the process of change, the same principles apply:

Smart answers to tough questions

Q: My head hurts. All this talk about soft stuff like people is worrying me. Can't you give me something easier to understand? Perhaps something more formulaic?

A: Absolutely. How about this:

$$SC = V + N + M + R + F$$

In other words, *Successful Change* requires a shared *Vision*; a compelling *Need* for change; the practical *Means* have been planned and introduced; the *Reward* systems have been aligned with the desired outcome to encourage the behaviors that will bring it about and *Feedback* is given regularly.

From *Managing the Change Process*, Carr, Hard & Trahant, McGraw-Hill

Awareness

- know what you want

- know where you are.

Alignment

- change your behaviors, your systems and your attitudes until they are in alignment with what you want

- maintain awareness to help track your progress

- work with what works; learn from and discard what doesn't.

We begin with raising awareness.

4

Raising Organizational Awareness

PART 1: VISION-MAKING
Raising awareness of the organization as it could be

'Too many organizations ask us to engage in hollow work, to be enthusiastic about small-minded visions, to commit ourselves to selfish purposes, to engage our energy in competitive drives. Those who offer us this petty work hope we won't notice how lifeless it is ...'

A Simpler Way, Wheatley & Kellner-Rogers

The word 'vision' conjures up images of a wide-eyed leader with flowing hair and a background of Holst, going 'I've got it, I've got it!' when he clearly isn't going to be able to pass on what he's got to anyone else in the world.

The vision stage is not about life-changing breakthroughs on the Road to Damascus. It is about seeing the organization in its intended changed state, free of the current inhibitors and blockages.

Vision is one of the most uncomfortable, least understood, most fudged and most dismissed areas of change management, mostly because people think that painting such a picture of the future state makes you unrealistic or pie in the sky. This misses the point of Vision, which is not to show an unfeasibly perfect future, but *to work out how you can get there.*

A vision should paint an attractive, energizing picture of the organization in the changed state, embodying the values and practices it wants to have. This allows a group to see how they'll know the change has been successful: 'when the world is like the vision, we'll know we've arrived.'

The vision, showing this idealized state, then presents an implication – what do we have to change in order to get there?

I've found a good exercise for the vision-creating group is actually to reverse that question and ask it as if it were already in the ideal world. So the question becomes: 'what did we have to do to get here?'

Answering that question requires working backwards, not forwards., and following a path, step by logical step, into the present. What you'll then find is your first stepping stone in front of you – the first thing you must do to make the dream become real – and a trail of steps into the future.

This trail of action is general and directional, not specific. Detailed analysis and agreement over what and how to do it can be carried out later.

Turning the invisible into the visible:
ten things a vision must do

- A vision must imply direction (where), purpose (why) and strategy (how).

- A vision must present a bold goal that explains and justifies the change the goal must stretch the organization beyond its current reality and take it to a higher level of aspiration.

- A vision must be relevant to the identity of the company, or justify a change.

- A vision must be real – even it stretches the organization beyond even its current levels of perception, it must have elements of current reality e.g. recognizable values, principles or competencies.

- A vision must be outward-looking – i.e. focused on a business and/or customer objective.

- A vision must attract commitment – by clearly implying the (pain and) pleasure of (not) changing.

- A vision must be understandable in terms of everyone's job – how will it affect them?

- A vision must speak to the head and the heart – stir emotions as well as ideas.

- A vision must be an 'awful attractor', i.e. it provokes or scares people as well as entices them.

- A vision must use vivid, powerful language. You'll never be able to say exactly what each word means in the vision itself (words just aren't like that) – but your language should be strong enough to stimulate questions and discussion. Above all, you need to know what the words mean. If someone asks you: 'So we're going to be a *formidable* competitor, eh? What will we be doing that makes us formidable?' – you'll need to be able to tell them, exactly. See Chapter 5 for communicating for shared understanding.

If your vision statement is very short, (the advertising agency St Luke has a vision which is two words long: *Open Minds*), then of course it won't be able to encapsulate all ten points above in the words alone. But you should be able to explain that the words you have chosen are relevant and meaningful. Imagine your vision statement as a hypertext linked document: each word in it should be just one click away from a meaningful definition or explanation. Visions should be rich and have depth ('a 3-D scratch and sniff model'), because they need to connect with hearts and spirit as well. Visions will die if they are flat and bland and connect only with the intellect.

Smart quotes

'If your intention is clear, you create an electric field of possibility that actually pulls creativity out of yourself and those around you. This is the real power of intention. It inspires you in ways you could not predict. When Kamatsu developed their intention – Encircle Caterpillar – they did not know exactly how they were going to do it. Far from it, in fact. One of the hallmarks of a good intention is that it should be bigger than your current abilities. As their clarity with this intention grew, they found themselves devising technology and marketing strategies commensurate with the size of their intention ... Growth is an excitement in individuals and companies and comes from stretching to achieve things that may not have seemed possible even a week earlier.'

From *The Corporate Mystic*, Gay Hendricks

More than just a list of statements: six ways of embodying your vision

- a vision as a video

- a vision as a story

- a vision as a hypertext-linked, graphics-heavy web site

Q: Where do values fit in all of this?

A: Perhaps your vision turns out to be a list of values – a values statement. Values guide behavior and I don't know and can't conceive of a high-performance team which doesn't set out its own internal rules of engagement. You can't rely on predicting the future, or the intensity or scope of changes that the universe is going to throw at you, but you ought to be able to rely on the fact that you share with your team a set of common beliefs or principles that govern (nine times out of ten) your reaction to change.

If you lead a team, I recommend you produce a set of values you aspire to in every activity you're asked to perform. Some suggestions on what makes a value:

A value is not a value unless it has seven factors:

- it must be freely chosen
- it must be chosen from a consideration of alternatives
- it must be chose with clear knowledge of the consequences
- it must be prized and cherished
- it must be publicly proclaimed
- it must be acted upon
- it must be acted upon repeatedly.

Simon & Kirschenbaum: *Values Clarification*

Smart answers to tough questions

- a vision as a collage or painting

- a vision as a sculpture

- a vision as a 'corporate brochure' for the new-world company – with a chairman's statement, results and pictures.

'Even if there is no point [to life], even if it is all a game of science, we must still believe that there is a point. If we don't believe that, there will be no reason to do anything, believe anything, change anything. The world would then be at the mercy of all those who do believe that they could change things. It is a risk we cannot run.

'To find that point ... it helps to build on three senses:

A Sense of Continuity
'We need to have a faith in the future to make sense of the present, [a] cathedral philosophy, the thinking behind the people who built the cathedrals, knowing that they would never live long enough to see them finished. The new cathedrals will not be of stone and glass, but of brains and wits ...

A Sense of Connection
'We need to belong, to someone or something. Only when there is a mutual commitment will you find people prepared to deny themselves for the good of others. Duty and conscience have no meaning if there is no sense of commitment to others ...

A Sense of Direction
'We need to believe in what we are doing if we are to lift ourselves on to a second curve [of renewal], or if we are going to compromise our wishes and needs for the good of others. There could be a stage beyond [Maslow's] self-realization, a stage which we might call idealization, the pursuit of an ideal or a cause which is more than oneself ...'

From *The Empty Raincoat*

A vision doesn't just offer a target or a goal. It is wider and deeper than that. Vision offers a 'Reason for Being' even though the future cannot be predicted ... but what constitutes a Reason for Being?

Perhaps if you really want to build a vision that encapsulates not just business objectives but gives a sense of human meaning and purpose, you could compare your vision statement with Charles Handy's Three Senses (see the smart quote from *The Empty Raincoat* on p. 68).

(see the smart quote from *The Empty Raincoat* on p. 68).

There is one more reason why vision-making is a good idea. Vision is declared intention – it allows everyone to be clear on what the point of the work of the company is, and allow them the chance to match their personal values with that purpose (if they can't they'll leave).

Smart quotes

'It is not what the vision is, but what it does that matters.'

Peter Senge

Joining in the making of it is an powerful, communal affirmation that the goal is worth striving for. Every work force will be happy to tell you just how awful things are – human beings are very able to focus on the negative; but if the group cannot work together to envision a better future, then change is going to be very difficult.

Sharing in the creation of the vision is not just democratic and respectful, it can release much-needed positive energy for the change.

To a positive, creative work force which is willing to take responsibility for change, the vision stage can provide much-needed purpose, context and meaning.

To a cynical, antagonistic work force, your vision is likely to be seen as rhetoric, hot air, propaganda, sloganeering.

For both sets of stakeholders, one principle above all else is true. There is no way round this one:

You must walk your talk.

In other words, in order to prove that your vision is not just pie in the sky, that your values are not just nice-sounding words, you have to lead your way in showing – in your behavior – what you mean. You must begin to embody the change.

A measure of your success would be this:

Smart things to say about change

> This is how I'd like to see it happen. A new customer or supplier comes to meet our company for the first time. The discussion comes round to the cultural change program we're undergoing. He asks us what the Vision is. Instead of getting a framed piece of paper down off the wall, we take him to see a particular group or activity. 'This', we say, 'is how we are trying to make our vision real.'

This making of reality is the function of alignment. But there is other work to do yet.

Beyond vision

'*A man is sweeping the floor, when all of a sudden, he reaches Enlightenment.*

'*What does he do? He continues to sweep the floor.*'

Buddhist principle

'After enlightenment, the laundry.'

Zen saying

So now you have your vision – and people are not exactly falling over themselves to change just yet.

What will help you next will be to give your people a clear, real, undeniable picture of where they are now – and then prove to them that this reality is no longer acceptable.

You need to move to the Analysis stage.

PART TWO: ANALYSIS
Raising awareness of the organization as it is

The word 'analysis' conjures up images of beardy statisticians pouring over sheets and sheets of data and going 'hmm, fascinating!' when it's clearly not going to be fascinating to anyone else in the world.

The analysis stage is not about number-crunching. The analysis stage is about seeing things as they are – not better, not worse, just as they are. It is

Smart quotes

'If we want to change what has come into form, we need to explore the self that has created what we see. A self changes when it changes its consciousness about itself. As the system develops a different awareness, this changed awareness will materialize as new responses. If it fails to assign different meaning, it will maintain itself unchanged.'

Margaret Wheatley and Myron Kellner-Rogers, *A Simpler Way*

about raising awareness of and in the organization, so that it can be pulled into change, either through reacting against and moving *away from* what it finds it dislikes, or creating a clear path *towards* the vision.

The analysis stage gathers a clear picture of the organization as it stands at the moment in all its glory and shame. You want to know what its current values and beliefs are (as opposed to those it prints in the brochure); how it feels about change and the future; what its skills and abilities are, apparent and hidden; what has happened in the past that may help or hinder the current plan; its rumors, fears and doubts; its glaring weaknesses; a view on the heroes and villains; its ability to communicate, internal and externally; its attitude to those who lead it; its attitude to your initial change ideas.

You can use:

- forum groups

- culture audits (one-on-one or small group surveys)

- informal chats in the pub

- formal interviews with customers/suppliers/family members

- the evidence of your own six senses.

Decide which are the main areas of the organization you wish to find out about. From which half dozen perspectives do you wish to consider it?

Here are the main headings from a culture audit questionnaire which seeks information in seven key areas:

Seven dimensions of corporate culture

1. Climate

    how it feels to work here; how the group feels about itself

2. Focus

    perceptions of the purpose and strategy of the group

3. Leadership and management

    attitude towards those who direct and manage the group

4. Structure

    how the group organizes itself to meet business requirements

5. Resources

    the capability the group has to deliver what is required of them

6. Personal development

    its attitude to the growth and remuneration of its people

7. Customer

    the group's attitude to those it serves.

Information gathered from an audit like this has many benefits:

- It can identify and focus on those areas of culture which are strong and those which are weak – and understand why.

- Some themes or trend appear that cross all the areas. In one audit I carried out recently, it was quite clear that all areas of the culture, and therefore performance, suffered from having no clear direction.

- It can identify which are going to be the best levers to use for improving things and with which priority. In the above example, the customer-care line needed investment in training, but that would have been only a temporary fix without sorting out the corporate direction first.

- It can be used to measure and regulate progress.

- Finally, a wealth of qualitative information also emerges from an audit which provides the 'warts and all' view of the organization. An audit builds not just a picture of the shared organizational beliefs and attitudes, but its strengths of feeling in key areas. This allows you to plan your communication and commitment strategies to limit resistance.

What to do now

- Gather the material and peruse it over a period of time. Don't rush.

- Be careful not to decide up-front what you want or expect to find. If you do, you'll find yourself sub-consciously filtering the information so that it fits your assumptions.

- Look for patterns and themes at this stage. In general, what would you say the main problems are that your analysis throws up? Don't worry

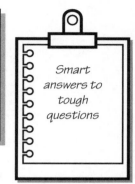

Smart
answers to
tough
questions

Q: Which comes first: the vision or the analysis?

A: If you do the analysis before creating a vision and expressing a commitment to making it real, you are in danger of becoming disillusioned by the amount of bad news that a truly 'warts and all' analysis may gather. Then again, doing the vision without a sense of how badly you need it might mean that the vision is either too tame, unrealistic, or misdirected. So there you are. I'd choose the chicken. No, the egg.

about justifying your hunches just yet – often your first impressions turn out to be correct.

- Write your conclusions page first, and only as bullet points.

- Only use the facts later to test these headlines.

- Reflect on your conclusions: do they speak to you with the ring of truth?

- Now write your report – remembering its purpose. I'm assuming here that you've spotted the need for change and that you work in an organization that needs some written verification for your decisions. But what is your report for? The report will give you air cover from top leadership,

Smart quotes

'Addiction is not just about drugs; it can occur in any behavior pattern when that behavior has become habitual (that is, routine, repetitive, without conscious control or full awareness). Change is natural and only painful if previous addiction has occurred – that is previous awareness was blunted. The pain is reduced if awareness can be extended progressively within a relationship of trust.'

Tony Page, *Diary of a Change Agent*

recruit change sponsors or champions, free up budget or permission. Make sure it makes clear what you want. Don't let the report be a way of your clarifying your thoughts and feelings (although a very early draft is OK for that). The report is not for you, it is for its audience and for the future of the change program. A report is to generate action.

How to write a report that gets action rather than filed

- Make it easy to read. 'Easy' in today's world means few pages, not short words, but if your case needs more than half a dozen pages, write compact paragraphs. Give plenty of sub-headings, to aid direction and clarity.

- Put a management summary – a one-page summary of the entire report – up-front.

- Put a one-page conclusion at the back, which summarizes the main findings and gives bullet-pointed action items for agreement.

- Consider binding your report, with a color logo, perhaps, or a suitable image or cartoon on the front page. Packaging catches the eye.

- Consider *not* binding your report. Leave it bare. Encourage the reader to copy and distribute amongst agreed other decision-makers.

- Write your headings and sub-headings for impact – they should be a headline for the main points under it.

- Back your case up with (anonymous) verbatim quotes from your interviews.

- Make it personal – minimize the use of the impersonal or passive cases. Say 'I felt that ...' rather than 'It was felt that ...'

- Especially make it personal when it comes to your conclusions. Who, in your opinion should do what and why? 'Rebecca Smith in Sales is best placed to ...' rather than 'the Sales Department should be charged with the task of ...'

- If you have to have statistics or graphs, stick them in the back where they belong. The majority of people you'll be selling your report to have got where they are today from being analytical, which is fine, but statistics are notoriously slippy and illusive. You don't want your audience to make up their own minds what your numbers mean and then not read the rest of the report.

- Make it abundantly clear what you want to mean. Don't leave anything open to interpretation – even those points you consider 'obvious'. Remember – if someone doesn't want to hear what you're saying, nothing is obvious.

- To clarify meaning, use lots of ' this means that ...'; 'the implication is ...'

- Make it easy for the person reading it to give a clear response (clear means either 'yes', 'no' or 'tell me more about X specifically and then I'll say yes'). Is it abundantly clear what the reader has to do as a result of reading the report? Does he or she need to:

  - grant permission?

  - enrol as a change sponsor?

- free-up budget or resources?

- communicate the decisions to anyone else?

- Deliver the report personally and set a date to discuss it; follow up to check when it's going to be read; follow up again to hear initial feedback after it has been read and confirm the date of the face-to-face meeting.

- And above all:

Write what you think and feel to be true. Don't fudge, apologize or hide (but if you don't know, say so). Stand by what you mean. It may feel dangerous, but the only way to start building trust is to be authentic, to be honest. If you don't feel a little anxious about how people are going to react when they read it (e.g. 'they might sack me for this!'), then in all probability you are not being provocative enough. Provocation isn't about taunting someone or exaggerating your points. Provocation – from the Latin *pro vocare* – calls some one forward and away from their current position. The only way to do this is to tell the truth, even if the truth hurts you and others.

> **Smart things to say about change**
>
> If we don't face up to the truth about what needs to change, we'll be choosing death. It may be a slow death, but die we will.

Beyond analysis

Vision – declared intention – is purpose, and analysis is clarity. But neither of these are a guarantee of success until everything you do is in alignment with what you want, and no longer in alignment with what you have and don't want.

> *RUNNING OS3*
>
> *(with thanks to Peter Sole, Wentworth Research)*
>
> - OS3 is a wonderful piece of software that doesn't have any bugs and doesn't make Bill Gates any richer.
> - OS3 is a piece of software that you already have in your mind and can be used whenever you want to test any report or conclusion (say at the end of a workshop).
> - OS3 works very simply:
>   Ask
>   os1: if our competitors got hold of a copy of this report (or these work-shop action points), would they say 'Oh shit! We're in trouble now because these actions mean they are really getting their act together.'
>   os2: if your spouse or partner read this report, would she say 'Oh shit – you'd better start looking for a new job/get ready for a serious promotion, because this report kicks ass (or insert appropriate descriptor if spouse or partner is not American)!'
>   os3: if your team mates got hold of this report would they say: 'Oh shit, its the same old same old. Nothing's going to change, again.'
> - Keep running the software throughout iterations of the report-writing until the questions produce two firm 'yesses' and a solid 'no' (in that order).

Talk can be cheap. There are no shortage of companies who *say* that their people are their greatest asset; the number who can prove it is very small. Be smart. Join that group.

Alignment closes the gap between intention and failure.

The following chapters show how you can make your visions real by aligning your communication, culture and measures in a learning environment of continuous, people-oriented change.

5

Aligning the Organization: Part 1

COMMUNICATING FOR CONSENSUS

'Communication is not simple ... and the revelation of its hidden complexity is one of the great discoveries of the twentieth century ... One sure sign of this complexity is our ignorance.'

Dr P.N. Johnson-Laird

In an early version of this book, I was going to call this chapter 'Change Tools: Number 1: Communication'. Then I realized that I couldn't think of tool number 2. Or 3. Why? Because, once you've used your mind to interpret how you should respond to the changing world and used your heart to tell you where you are now, communication is the *only* tool you have for changing your company.

There is nothing that you do which is not communicating something to somebody. You cannot cause anything to happen without communicating. This sounds glib and patronizing, but it's true.

You'd think therefore that we'd be masters of communication by now – but we aren't. You'd think we'd have a wonderful understanding of the vagaries of communication. But we don't.

This explains why so many change programs struggle or fail (or struggle and then fail).

Five principles for success in building consensus for change

(i) Involvement

Ownership is all. Do everything you can to include your people in the change process. Since they'll be implementing the vision, it borders on the immoral not to give your people the opportunity to shape it. Explain the problem, then ask for ideas, ask for feedback. Encourage them to challenge your decisions if that is what they feel they need to do – not only will this help you shape your strategy more precisely, it will also tell you what the nature of resistance is towards this project. If you have information about the project, give it away to them. You'll get back credibility. If you don't have information about the project, tell them so. In return you'll gain trust.

(ii) Education

Explain why you have decided to take the route you are taking; explain what other choices you did *not* take and why; explain what the context is that has shaped these decisions; explain how other companies are making the same sorts of changes (thus preventing too much 'grass is always greener on the other side' mentality); explain the benefits and the anticipated costs; explain what new policies will be put in place to support the change; explain what you believe the change will mean, positive and negative, to every single person in the group.

(iii) Honesty

Above all, tell the truth; that way you don't have to remember what you said. Some people will react to the proposed change with fear, and will employ a series of conscious and subconscious strategies to attempt to counter it. If stress is high, this web of avoidance and dark side behavior will get very messy; in the worst cases, change programs can be like building on sand. You need, (and everyone else needs) a firm foundation: the truth.

(iv) Congruency

'Congruency' is another word for alignment, which is another way of saying 'walk your talk', and could be more formally termed 'behavior modelling'. Leaders are expected to be good speakers, and like politicians, we know that they can spin a good story – that's how they got to be where they are. What makes consensus more likely is in seeing that talk is matched by the individual actions of the speaker, so that he or she becomes a living example of the intention. Leaders can also create this congruency at an organizational level, by sending what Mark Youngblood calls 'symbolic shockwaves ... radical actions that demonstrate unequivocally that the change effort is for real.' The CEO who called a company-wide meeting in the car park of his tyre factory, and, when the crowd was gathered, said nothing, but took off his jacket and set about the pile of rejected, shoddilymade tyres with an axe – that CEO was sending a symbolic shockwave that his previous week's speech about TQM was in earnest.

(v) Persistence

Change takes time, and people forget what was said at the change project-launch. Persistence has at least three dimensions:

- *creativity* – to maintain people's interest

- *reassurance* – to tend to their changing emotional condition as they pass through transition; and

- *reinforcement* – repeating the same message consistently and testing for understanding of it in their words and action.

Spiral pyramids: a new way of looking at communication

As Richard Nixon famously said, 'I know you believe you understood what you think I said, but I'm not sure you realize what you heard is not what I meant to say ...'

Communication is perhaps the most overused word in business. Everyone knows that it matters – I've never yet met a company which didn't think it had a communication problem – and in fact it tends to get blamed for everything ('communication is everyone's panacea for everything', Tom Peters). But who actually knows what it is? Like US Supreme Court Justice Steven's famous definition of pornography ('I know it when I see it'), we all recognize communication when it happens to us. However, its significance and our need to control and manage it demands that we do better than just know it when we see it. We need to be able to define it so that we

I was CEO of a small manufacturing company in the Midlands. I reckoned I was a man of principle and fairness. Above all I decided to be honest about the impact of the recession – about our falling revenues, the forthcoming changes and why they were necessary for our company. I thought that telling the truth was the simplest option. How could I fail, I thought, if I was honest?

So I called a company-wide meeting – I wanted everyone to hear what I had to say at the same time, so there could be no chance of rumor-mongering. That was a huge affair – we had to get in emergency cover. And I told them the truth: that no redundancies were planned and that 'everyone would be treated as fairly as possible.'

To my dismay, this meeting started a wildfire of rumors about plant closures and lay-offs. Productivity fell. Morale plummeted. It was almost the opposite impact to what I'd intended.

After months of investigations and a year of hindsight, we realized what had happened. Never before had there been a company-wide meeting on *any* issue. It was such a change to the standard way of doing things that they began to make up justifications for it. My audience inferred that things must have got really bad to merit such a big meeting and that there was probably 'more to it' than I presented. In other words, they thought I was covering up. They decided I was lying, even though I was telling the truth.

It was very strange and very scary.

CEO, Rubber Company (retired)

can identify its elements and its force and functions. We need to know what it looks like, and then, perhaps we can master it as a management tool.

We need a standpoint from which to structure our intuitive understanding that communication is messy, complex and dangerous.

The old model of communication

There are familiar, traditional models – but these are not adequate for our purpose. What is the current communication model used by most management professionals? In general it is a version of a model created by telecommunication scientists half a century ago (Shannon and Weaver, 1949). It has these elements: a transmitter, identified as a source for the communication, issuing a message to a receiver. The simple model looks like this:

A sophistication of the model adds an element of feedback:

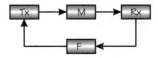

It is this image which dominates our thinking about communication. It's been a sturdy model – it serves a purpose, and if it ain't broke, why fix it? Well, it is broke. It has these faults:

The terminology is all wrong

We are not just transmitters and we are certainly not mere receivers of data. That's fine for telephones, but rather a limited perspective for people. When the Chief Executive tells his employees that he 'believes in people' what they receive is considerably more than that simple message – they interpret the plain data in the shadow of his and his executives' past behavior, his other statements, networks of rumor, their own prejudices, the relative size of his company car against theirs, and so on.

None of this is intrinsic to the message 'I believe in people', yet all this, and more, may be interpreted into it. Every time someone says, 'I thought I made that clear', or 'you should have understood that', we acknowledge that the message is not the meaning. Somehow, in all the consideration of how well it flows, we have missed out the concept of how effective our communication has been.

The elements are in the wrong place

The old model defines the transmitter and the receiver as conceptually separate. This encourages us to think that we are rendered safe by distance from our audience. We are not. In Phillip Clampitt's terms, this is the 'Arrow approach', and 'arrow managers never know if they are "on target" or not.' (*Communicating for Managerial Effectiveness*, Newbury Park, 1991.) They just assume that they are.

Talk to anyone, send them a letter even – and you are, for that moment, in an intimate and often exclusive relationship with them. There is no escape from an audience. In fact, every audience is transmitting strong signals to the presenter of the form: 'I am bored' or 'I am attentive' or 'I am confused' or 'I am hot'. In receiving this information, the presenter constantly interprets his audience. So every 'receiver' is also a 'transmitter' and vice versa. We are always both. This has profound implications for change leaders who think that their job is simply 'to keep people informed.' In fact, their job should be far more two-way than that.

It's the wrong kind of system

The old model is a closed system which suggests that communication has no external inputs and that when we communicate we effectively get back to where we started. This neglects the influence of the context on any communication – to smile during a firing has rather a different value from the same act during a hiring. It also neglects the possibility of development in a transactional relationship. As soon as two parties begin to communicate, they begin to share facts and impressions with each other which will mean that all further communication exists in a changed context. If I tell you my name is David and you tell me yours is Bob, we haven't moved round in a circle. We've added to the amount of information in the world and can never go back to the original point.

It's the wrong kind of feedback

There are two problems with the application of feedback in this model. First of all, feedback is not a box. It is a category error to treat it as qualitatively similar to the transmitter and receiver. Feedback is actually a force which impels the continuation of the process – it doesn't belong in a box: in practice it is the line. Secondly, a feedback mechanism requires reflexivity: it registers the actual state of a system, compares it to the desired state, then uses the comparison to correct the state. The old model makes no allowance for this sort of meta analysis where one has to hold simultaneously the propositions: 'this is my message' and 'this is their interpretation of my message.' As the aphorism goes: 'I am not what I think I am. I am not what you think I am. I am what I think you think I am.'

***

So the old model is deeply flawed. It is both obsolete and dangerously narrow in scope, with an excessive concentration on process and flow and precious little attention given to effectiveness and meaning. The result is that most management attempts to control or improve communication have concentrated on regulating the channels, the flow and the lines: 'who should communicate with whom, in what channel, at what frequency?' This is all entirely valid, but still fails to acknowledge the root issue of what is being communicated, how and with what effect.

It is the two missing factors, effectiveness and meaning, excluded from the old model, which are the key to any communication strategy. We need a new model which allows us to understand and manage the real issues.

A New Model of Communication

So what does communication look like, if it's not a circuit of boxes? Actually, it looks like a pyramid in a helix. It is a three-dimensional structure with two core elements – the Spiral and the Pyramid.

The Spiral

The players in the communication process are the performer and the audience – terminology which gives a far better reflection of the intrinsic human drama in communication. The performer issues a message, not directly to the audience but through the interpretative medium of some kind of reality or external context. It does arrive at the audience eventually. The model recognizes that at this point both audience and performer share the intimacy of connection – the role they each perform is essentially the same: that of interpreting the message.

Finally, as the message is reconceived by the audience, both actors in the transaction are at a new stage in the communication process – they have a wider shared knowledge field as they get more and more information about each other's points of view, personality traits, the topic etc. This is the feedback element of the model – an ever-widening helix of understandings which is charged with an energy and constantly developing. The helical structure illustrates the dynamic and transactional nature of communication and its development over time. It emphasizes that the elements, relationships and environments of the process are constantly changing, and irreversible. You can't go back down the spiral. You can't uncommunicate, as many leaders have found to their cost.

The Pyramid

It is not enough to understand the process – we need also to understand the underlying purpose and impact. We need to recognize that the message itself is a construction of elements, or signs, which, through their interaction with the performer and audience, produce meanings. These signs can be anything from one's state of dress to the tone of one's voice, including, but not dominated by, the words one has chosen. The message then, is not just something issued by the performer to the audience, but a part of a structured relationship with the other two points of the triangle. The emphasis is not on the 'content' of the message, but on how it is 'read' by its audience and performer as they bring their values and experiences to bear on it. This process of 'reading' the message is, in effect, a negotiation – the performer and the audience both generate a meaning from the message. The performer issues his message coded with an understanding of the context and the impact from his or her perspective. The audience does the same thing, but from its perspective. This is a complementary, parallel process, but is not identical.

As an example, take the phrase 'just do it'. This is often intended by its performers to be an inspirational challenge to cut through the 'administrivia' supported by the positive connotations of the Nike commercials. My context, however, as audience, includes strong negative connotations from a former colleague of mine. He used this phrase as a weapon to stifle debate and enforce his view on the group: 'don't argue, just do it'. I have taken the message, reflected it through my cultural experiences in reality, and generated a meaning. It requires work on my part to suppress that understanding and generate a compatible meaning with that which I assume the original performer has generated and intends – work which audiences are not always motivated to undertake. This sort of tangle is a feature of all communication, which takes place not at a logical level of data transfer but in deep in the pool of human psychological complexity.

As in any negotiation, then, the two parties need not share a similar result, though their aspiration is usually to advance to one. The performer's 'meaning' may well be dramatically different from the audience's. This points to an understanding of the dangers and confusions in communication. It also points to the inevitability of this assigning of meaning. We cannot live outside these readings. Indeed, meaning-generation, or the delight we take in sticking labels on things, should alert us to the fundamental insistency of communication in our lives. You can't step out of the pyramid. You can't not communicate.

Putting the two models together gives us the pyramid in the spiral:

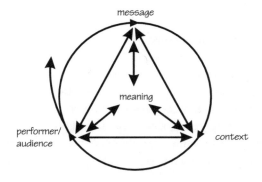

or, more dynamically, a tetrahedron in a helix:

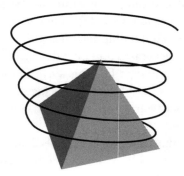

An extended version of this piece was written by Alan Leigh (ALeigh@exchange.ml.com) and originally published in Facilities Management '95 by Strathclyde Graduate School of Business.

The Power of the Pyramid/Helix Model: people come first not last in change

What is the significance of this model, what is its relevance to management in business, and in particular, what bearing does it have on communicating for change?

There are eight main conclusions:

- The world is a construction of texts and signs which are interpreted and given meaning by an audience over time. In other words, we have to try to influence those interpretations by the way in which we communicate, but we ultimately cannot control them. This is a huge shift in power from traditional communication models and from traditional ways of communicating in hierarchical organizations. The shift is from performer to audience.

- There is no substitute for getting close to your audience, communicating live, face-to-face, in small groups, so that you can see in real time how your message might be being interpreted. Distance communication (emails, memos, posters, podium speeches) plays its part, but true communication happens up-close

- Communication is a service transaction. We live in a world where every communication is the provision of a service to an audience/customer with the power to buy or not to buy our message and meaning. We should invest as much time, money, imagination and care into our corporate communications as we do into our advertising or PR. The Spiral Pyramids model suggests a way of communicating which puts the audience and its possible interpretations first: it is *audience-* (as in customer) *oriented*.

- Although we have huge control over how we design and shape our communications ultimately the audience decides what they mean. No matter how beautifully articulated our Vision, for example, their fear about its implications might cause them not to connect and commit with it. To truly communicate we have to care as much about the audience as our message.

- If we are serious about communicating well, as a matter of course, *before* we communicate, we must analyze every element of our message and ask 'how will this be interpreted?' and 'how do they need me to behave in order to generate the meaning which I would like them to generate?' This is not the vanity of the self-conscious, but the prudence of the aware.

- *After* communication we must always check to see what meanings were generated, how we were interpreted. Part of the impact of communication is seen in how people think, talk and behave as a result of it, but it is also necessary to make formal and informal checks of interpretation, just as we do formal 'courtesy calls' with our customers to check that our service is up to scratch. This is not about seeking praise for a good performance, but part of a never ending process of trying to understand your people better – what their needs are and how they are adapting to the change over time. With this approach, 'resistance' is reduced as you go.

- It is impossible to 'fail to communicate'. We can only fail to sell our version of the communication as we intend it. When companies admonish themselves for failing to communicate, they usually respond by increasing the *quantity* of communications. This will only help in some cases, because what they really mean by 'we failed to communicate' is 'our people didn't understand our messages in the way that we intended and therefore we didn't get the results we wanted.' The first wise response here should be to understand the needs of the audience better, not bombard it with more information.

- You cannot not communicate. Even absence communicates – i.e. is interpreted by an audience. That's why those change leaders who think that not giving people information in sensitive times is the safest option are playing a dangerous game. Silence is deafening. Audiences hate vacuums, and they fill it with their own interpretations of what might be communicated. When leaders stay quiet, the rumor mill gets loudest.

Communication: the hard–soft issue

It's astonishing to me that many managers still consider communication a soft issue, or a luxury, or a non-core activity. In fact, the soft issue of building trust through audience-oriented communication – by putting yourself in their shoes, thinking from their perspective – is done for a very specific reason: so that conflicts can be resolved as they arise. The irony is that the only way to resolve conflicts is to face them head on; it involves confronting uncomfortable opinions, hearing honest feedback, tackling some negative emotions, going into unsafe territory. That's not a soft, but a hard issue.

Communication comes from a Latin verb, *communicare*, which means 'to share'. Audience-oriented communication shares power between speaker and listener, so that the meaning can be negotiated openly and as cleanly as possible. Unequal power undermines organizations. As Rosabeth Moss Kantor put it, paraphrasing Lord Acton,

Powerlessness corrupts. Absolute powerlessness corrupts absolutely.

Audience-oriented communication is based on respect for the listener, for their opinions, their beliefs and their feelings. For the sake of the vision, all three of these things may have to shift in the listener, but the starting point needs to be one of respect and care, otherwise resistance really will kick in. People don't resist change, but truly resist being changed by unthinking others.

Audience-oriented communication identifies issues and blockers to change (misunderstanding, fear, unresolved bitterness, etc.) and does not avoid them. Why? Because the audience-oriented performer knows that only when these things are resolved or willingly set aside can progress towards commitment be made.

Communicating change: the essential questions that your audience asks

- Is the alternative to *not* changing *painful* enough to cause me to react against it?

- Is the outcome of the vision *pleasurable* enough to draw me towards it?

- What will I actually have to *do* differently; how will my working day change?

- How and who will I be working with?

Smart answers to tough questions

Q: So what you're saying is that communication is a nightmarishly complicated and never-ending process? But how much communication is enough? Is there a point at which we can say we've got our message across in the way we intended?

A: When people tell you to stop communicating so much with them; when they tell you that the amount of communication has more than served its purpose of attitude adjustment and information sharing, and is now beginning to get in the way. Otherwise, keep communicating until you meet your own objective for the communication, and that comes down to setting a goal for every piece of communication. In other words, ask yourself, 'what do I want my audience to do as a result of this communication? Do I want them to change their behavior? How? Change a belief? And how will I see or hear that?' Then, when your audience is meeting your objective, move on to communicating a new issue.

- What good will it bring me in terms of my career, my marketability, my value to this and other companies?

- What good will it bring me psychologically – growth, new skills, job satisfaction?

The 7× Rule

As an interesting rule of thumb, there is an old principle from way back, which suggests that in order to get anyone in an organization to understand anything, you have to tell them it 7 different times and in 7 different ways. If this 7× rule has any truth in it at all (and it usually provokes in my audiences that interesting mixture of *wow*! and *oh shit*! which leads me to suspect that it may well be correct), then it makes considerable demands on both your patience and your creativity. Do you have the reserves of persistence to keep telling them what you want them to hear enough times for them to 'get it'; and do you have the ingenuity to tell them the same message in enough varied and attention-grabbing ways for them to understand it?

Here, as many times, organizational communication takes on more and more of the qualities of advertising, and less and less of that dry, information-spewing mechanics we'd always imagined it to be. Advertising balances repetition and variety in order to get deep into the nodes of your brain, either so you'll go out and buy the product (i.e. change your behavior), or express an interest in getting more information about it (i.e. change your attitude).

Perhaps the mythically wacky and trendy advertising world has some intriguing lessons for us to transfer into corporate communication.

(You've got a week to compose a jingle. I want you all back in my office humming it by Friday.)

Maximizing use of communication channels

One way that you can ensure you're meeting the '7 different ways' element of the 7× rule is by making full use of the various channels of communication open to you.

Different communication channels have different qualities, and these will either help or hinder your message. Telephone conversations allow almost instant feedback but require the sender and receiver to be 'up' at the same time. They can allow for human warmth but lack formality, so it would be a shitty way to hear that you'd lost your job. Face-to-face meetings are almost always best for dealing with highly complex or emotionally charged situations. For exactly this reason, many people use the other communication channels to avoid the complexities of what they are doing. How many managers have hidden behind a memo?

Email has spread over our organizations like a rash because it fits the needs of organizations to have information quickly, cheaply, and to diminish problems caused by distance and time zones. Email is congruent with one of the predominant business values of this age: speed. The trouble is it's not great for dealing with emotion or for clarifying understanding, two of the major objectives when building commitment for change. I've witnessed untold damage done to change programs by hastily written emails sent off to huge audiences at the click of a mouse. With emails, once they're gone, they're gone. You'd think we'd have learnt to treat email with respect because of this truth, but the opposite seems to be true: because email's quick and easy, people often use it badly.

At the same time, when the new CEO was recently appointed at a major high-street retail organization, he used email deliberately to introduce himself and his intentions to the organization. Why? Because it was deliberately antithetical to the old culture – which would have sent round a highly formal letter to each member of staff. And because his message was about working together for the future and he knew email, for all its limitation, does reach a web of people instantly. When you receive an email that you can see from the distribution list has gone to every other person in the company, perhaps a part of you really does feel to be part of a greater community.

Remember then that email can be magnificent, but only in its place.

And what is its place? Eddie Obeng, in his *New Rules for the New World* (Capstone 1997), displays the use of channels graphically, along two axes: the emotional content on the vertical scale and the need to communicate interactively to deliver the result.

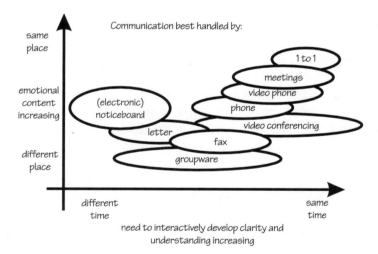

Connecting with your audience: the five dimensions of influence

You will not be long in your career as a smart change agent before you have to get up from behind the meeting table and present your recommendations to the group. You may even have to get up and present to the whole company. Even summarizing a report at a sit-down meeting is a presentation and needs just as much care and preparation. In all these cases, your job is to influence your audience to alter their attitude, awareness or behavior. Influence, therefore, is a key change tool.

Influence has five dimensions: each dimension responds to a question or questions that your audience is asking of you.

- *Intensity*

  How much does this subject seem to matter to you?

  How connected are you to your material?

- *Credibility*

  How natural and sincere are you?

  Are you being 'yourself'?

- *Orientation*

  Are you thinking about this problem from my perspective?

  Are you responding to my needs?

UCLA Professor Emeritus of Psychology who in the sixties carried out an experiment to prove the old theory, 'it's not what you say, it's the way that you say it'. That he was able to prove that the statement is no surprise, though the numbers are astonishing. Mehrabian says that 93% of the impact of any human communication is generated from the way that the words are said – 38% from the tone of voice used and the other 55% from visual cues. In other words, your audience is deciding whether to listen to the content based on whether it trusts your vocal tone and body language. If these two elements are not aligned with your words, they'll trust the 93% of *form* rather than the 7% of your *content*. People know when you are lying.

- *Mechanics*

Is anything in your body language, your visual age, or the physical setting distracting me?

- *Semantics*

Are you defining clearly what you mean?

Is your choice of words memorable and inspiring?

It's not what you *do* it's just how you do it
It's not what you *say* it's just how you say it
It's not what you *do* it's just how you do it
And that's what *gets* results.
(With thanks to *Bananarama*)

Smart things
to say about
change

Using delegation to create a new reality

It would be nice to think that raising awareness in organizations was considered a noble end in itself. But businesses are made as successful as they are by pragmatists (I choose that phrase carefully – 'as successful as they are', perhaps not as successful as they could be). In any case, at some point the talking has to stop.

Delegation is your change tool for creating a new reality – getting the idea out of your head, mixing it with the understanding and commitment that your presentation has generated in your colleagues, and birthing it in the world as action through others.

A Delegation checklist

'Hold yourself responsible for a higher standard than anyone expects of you.'

H.W. Beecher

Explain the purpose of the task

Connect little purpose to Big Purpose:

- why it's important to you and your plans

- why it's important to the company and its plans

- why it's important to the person being delegated to

- why it's suitable and fitting that this person does it.

Clarify the results you expect:

- what it will look like in your eyes

- **not** how you intend them to get there.

Define the authority level

- *Level 6.* Take action – no further contact with me required.

- *Level 5.* Take action – let me know what you did.

- *Level 4.* Look into it – let me know what you intend to do; do it unless I say 'no'.

- *Level 3.* Look into it – let me know what you intend to do; don't do it until I say 'yes'.

- *Level 2.* Look into it – let me know possible actions, include pros and cons of each and recommend one for my approval.

- *Level 1.* Look into it – report all the facts to me; I'll decide what to do.

Agree on a deadline

- Assert that you never set a deadline that you don't intend to keep and ask that they view this in the same light.

- Ask what they might, if necessary, be prepared to set aside (or delegate themselves) in order to meet this deadline.

Professor of Management Emeritus at the Sloan School of Management at MIT, Schein is widely regarded as creating he term 'corporate culture'. Certainly his book *Organizational Culture and Leadership* spawned a whole industry of books and research papers.

Schein developed Kurt Lewin's Unfreeze–Change–Refreeze model. At the unfreezing stage, Schein points out that giving up one's attitudes and habitual behavior is painful, as any loss is. Schein believes that three process are involved to generate the readiness to change:

1. *disconfirmation* by demonstrating the falsity of something held to be true and good
2. *inducing anxiety* by underlining how personally damaging that loss of truth is to the person
3. *providing psychological safety* to the extent that the person can accept that the new reality is inevitable.

In stage 2, change, people quickly try to bring back some stability to their lives, since the unfreezing stage brings significant insecurity. Schein suggests that two main mechanisms bring about this new stability:

- *identification with a role model*, whose own values and beliefs can be absorbed
- *a process of trial and error*, where the person exposes themselves to a wide range of experience and information.

If any of this sounds to you like the briefing manual of a trainee brainwasher, then you get full points for your perceptiveness; Schein was involved in the debriefing and repatriation of prisoners of war who had been held by the Chinese communists during the Korean War. 'There's nothing bad about brainwashing', Schein is reported to have said much later, 'it's the Communism that was bad.'

Schein's work has a number of implications for smart brainwashers, sorry, change agents:

- A great deal of work needs to be done in informing people why the 'old way' cannot and will not work any longer, perhaps as much if not more work than needs to be done in advocating the 'new way'. This is a difficult and sensitive task, because it induces pain in people, and is one that many would shy away from. It's easier to spend session after session extolling the virtues of the new world, because nobody's been there yet – there's little invested in it other than imagination. As such it's an impersonal, relatively safe task. Asking someone to give up the old world is tantamount to a personal attack – and too many people shy away from that.
- There are perhaps too many managers in old command-and-control cultures who actually would be quite comfortable with the disconfirmation stage; what many of us lack is the capacity for creating safe psychological space. Building trust and allowing difficult emotions to be expressed and explored may not be in your official job description, but it certainly has to be in your smart one.
- Walking your talk as a change leader puts you in place as an ideal role model for all those people walking about dazed in Schein's Change stage, looking for someone to believe in. The warning here, of course, is that they might hook up to another, entirely unsuitable role model. There's a great Dr Seuss children's story in which a baby bird hatches from her shell, falls straight out of the nest, and spends the next 40 pages believing that, consecutively, a dog, a cat, a cow, a plane and a mechanical digger must be her mother. What is not funny is that people in need of a new role model often connect with the loudest, strongest voices, and amidst organizational change, those who are regarded as 'resistors' and 'trouble-makers' might well have those dangerous, siren and powerfully attractive voices. Beware of their influence, and act decisively to counter it.
- Finally, Schein warns smart change agents that care has to be taken in the refreezing stage. Old behaviors and norms that still exist in the organization – or remind people of them – can pull people back to the pre-change state. (This is exactly what happens when you put yourself on a training course – you fill full of new skills and attitudes, and make a strong resolve to continue the improvement, but then find yourself gradually dragged down to everyone else's attitudinal level when you get back to work.) In your change work, eradicate as far as possible all reminders of old ways of

doing things – old systems, processes, procedures, even artifacts such as time sheets designed in the old way. And if you are leading a change within a group that is part of a larger one that is not going through the same change, then pay particular attention to the boundaries between your group and the larger one. Brief your people to expect and resist the influence of the old ways. And use your powers of *coercive persuasion* (the name of another book by Schein, incidentally) to get the larger group on board as soon as possible.

Obtain feedback

- Check understanding of the need.

- Check degree of commitment.

- Check ability to carry out the task.

- Deal with doubts, confusions or fears.

Provide for controls

- milestones towards the goal

- interim review points

- open door policy outside of these to bring up any doubts or concerns.

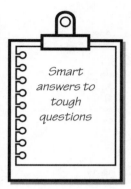

Q: So-and-so is being really destructive to this change program, being negative and cynical. It's really getting to the team, and particularly the more junior ones. What are you going to do about him?

A: I agree he's behaving in that way. I'll spend time with him this afternoon. I'll need him to know how I and others have been interpreting his behavior – he may not be fully aware of the impact he's having. If he is doing it deliberately, I'll ask him what he needs to know or feel in order to come on side with this change program – more information, for example, or training, maybe even career counselling. As far as is practical and in the spirit of the change, I'll give him that. When we've made that compact, he'll have an agreed amount of time to turn his behavior around. During that time I'll take time to make it clear how the old world he's supporting is not coming back and will not be tolerated. If the change doesn't happen, I'll make it clear that I'll be looking for ways to find him work in other areas of the organization. But the main point is that I'll give him every opportunity to change of his own accord. And in the meantime, I'll make an extra effort with the junior staff to explain that his behavior, whilst understandable, is inappropriate and not the future of this company. In that way, I'll make it abundantly clear what the implications are of aligning with him.

Smart answers to tough questions

Prepare for reward and recognition

- What can you do to publicly acknowledge success?

- Remind the audience who hears this public acknowledgment of the work's 'fit' in the context of the larger purpose.

- As far as possible match the reward to the person and the theme of the change.

6
Aligning the Organization: Part 2

BUILDING TRUST: THE TRUTH ABOUT RESISTANCE TO CHANGE

'He that is without sin among you, let him first cast a stone ...'

The Bible, St John, Ch. 8, v. 9

Leaders never resist change, of course. It's 'them'. 'They' do.

Resistance is an interesting word, reminiscent of the war, and suggestive that people in organizations have nothing better to do than plan secret guerrilla raids against change leaders. Smart change leaders need a more realistic, inquiring and sensitive stance towards the impact change has on people.

Resistance is a good thing

This chapter suggests that we do not need to 'overcome' resistance to change: the more we fight resistance, the more it'll probably fight back. ('What you resist persists', as God says in Neale Donald Walsch's *Conversations with God*). If change were about force and might, then such a metaphor might be an appropriate one. But change is not a battle. Change is about *helping* people adapt consciously from a status quo that no longer serves the company to a new world that will. If this provokes the behaviors which are traditionally labelled 'resistance', then this is a good thing, not a bad. Why? Four main reasons:

- It's a sure sign that the change has begun. When resistance surfaces it is because assumptions and beliefs are being challenged – the precursor to them being replaced with new ones.

- The resistance tells us that what we have tried is not working perfectly yet. Resistance is feedback. If we look beneath its surface, we'll find a wealth of information on what we need to do differently and better.

- Resistance is a programmed healthy response when continuity and evolution depends on it. If living organisms had no resistance to change, they'd probably keel over from continual adaptation. People who resist change are rarely trying to sabotage your efforts; rather they are trying to protect what they see to be right and valuable. Resistance allows you one more chance to review your change objectives against current reality. As we bring in the future, what of the past might stay to help us? A new broom is often required in organizations – but there is no need to throw the baby out with the bath water. Work with what works, whether that's new or old.

- Resistance is loyalty in action. The trouble is that the loyalty is towards something in the past – an old culture, a long-gone leader, or simply 'the way we're used to doing things around here'. Think positively: you have the tools to turn that misplaced loyalty into a loyalty that supports the change. You'd be in real trouble if your people weren't showing loyalty towards anything (in which case I'd ask again where your recruitment consultant goes on holiday).

What they say: the sound of resistance

Here are some things people say when they are apparently 'showing resistance':

- It's just another management fad.

- We've never done it like that.

- It can't be done like that.

- The customer won't like it.

- The technology can't do that.

- It would take too long.

- We don't have enough resources to do it.

- It won't work, you know.

- If you listen, I'll tell you how it could be done, but I know you won't listen so I won't bother.

Smart quotes

'There is no squabbling so violent as that between people who accepted an idea yesterday and those who will accept the same idea tomorrow.'

Christopher Morley, writer

'We will change ourself if we believe that the change will preserve our self.

'We are unable to change if we cannot find ourselves in a new version of the world.

'We must be able to see that who we are will be available in this new situation.'

From *A Simpler Way*

Thank goodness we've never made excuses like that, eh? That's because leaders never resist change, of course. It's 'them'. 'They' do.

Well we do. We all do. These behaviors and attitudes are common to all people. Everyone involved in this book – me, you, all the people whose work forms the basis for the ideas herein – has at some point tried to hide the fear they are feeling behind a bluff of bravado or stubbornness. These behaviors grow out of fairly fundamental fears – most of them to do with losing one's sense of identity.

What they mean when that's what they say ...

'I'm scared ...' and, more precisely:

1. 'Although I'm nodding, I don't understand – what you are intending, why you're doing it or how it will all happen. I'm not stupid, it's just that my fears and internal dialogue deafened me whilst you were explaining your ideas.'

What they'd say if they could:

'Empathize with me more. Tell me – in a way that I believe – that you understand my fears and have some ways to deal with them, before I have to understand your ideas.'

2. 'I do understand but I just don't think I can do it.'

What they'd say if they could:

'Explain to me clearly that you want me to stay and that you have considered that I am capable of the required change. At the moment I'm feeling a little vulnerable, so you'll have to tell me what you see in me that I'm failing to see at the moment.'

3. 'I think you'll get someone else in to replace me when it becomes evident that I can't do it.'

What they'd say if they could:

'Show me your plans for new hirings; what plans do you have for training me; is that committed/good enough to help me change or am I being set up to fail?'

4. 'My self-worth is not up to making these changes. I fear I may let myself and my loved ones down.'

What they'd say if they could:

'The scale of the changes appears huge to me; perhaps the stress I'm feeling is pushing me to get things out of proportion. I feel useless, past it. Tell me again that I can and will fit into the future of the company if

I try my best. Show me the productive ways I can try my best. Help me explain what's going on to my family, who have got used to me doing a certain job in a certain way.'

5. 'I do understand what you are saying and actually disagree for some very considered reasons.'

What they'd say if they could:

'Sorry. It's my lack of self-confidence that makes me talk in generalizations. But I really would like to tell you why I think you are wrong. However, I'm afraid of the consequences of getting into conflict with you (besides I'm just not very good at conflict). You'll have to help me understand that it's safe for me to speak up.'

Fears like these – and the behavior it generates – need compassion, not judgment.

Judgment tends to close things down. Suppose you decide it's their fault for not understanding? What are you going to do next? Where else can you go? All you've created is a wall of stubbornness. And walls (he said profoundly) have two sides ...

Compassion, on the other hand – recognizing that you too are often guilty of avoidance and self-justification – should lead you into discovering new ways forward. If, for example, they don't understand, it doesn't really matter whose fault it is. Whose problem is it, that's the good question. And the answer is: it's yours. So what else can you try? How else can you communicate your message which proves that you understand their concerns?

Ask:

- What's my part in this 'resistance'?

- What can I change in me to improve the situation?

What happens between what they mean and what they say ...
... and what you can do about it

When faced with a change or a communication that instills a fear reaction, the best thing someone could do is admit that they're afraid. But no-one ever does this; Ego does not allow it.

People are more likely to try one or more of the following avoidance tactics. These tactics are why change agents don't like resistance – and they tend to react to the surface behaviors rather than respond to what's going on underneath.

When faced with fear, people ...
... will too quickly come to a conclusion about what you mean

What you should do:

Take your time; be patient in explaining what you mean and what you don't mean (but what you suspect they want you to mean). Keep checking for understanding. Repeatedly ask for their questions.

... will filter what you say and select those fragments of information that support their fears and doubts

What you should do:

Listen to their statements and, where you suspect that they are latching on to only certain parts of what you've said, explain that they are missing other important truths. Take time over these.

... will supplement that information with other material from the corporate culture myth-bank and pseudo-history to 'prove' that you are mistaken, misguided or lying

What you can do:

Challenge them to realize that you are talking about the present and the future and not the past; where past company behavior or trends have been detrimental to your argument, explain clearly how you are overcoming that.

... will focus on and exaggerate the negative impact on them

What you can do:

Stress the positive individual and corporate benefits; make it clear that there are no options but to make this change; that discomfort is natural but negativity is not. Stress how you will help the former but not tolerate the latter

... will self-justify their behavior as common sense and natural

What you can do:

Empathize with their doubts but make it clear that it cannot be allowed to carry on unduly. Ask: what can I do to help minimize your discomfort?

... will move through the five stages of grieving

What you can do:

Allow it to happen; understand what's happening by reading on ...

Kubler-Ross, coming to terms with change

Dr Elisabeth Kubler-Ross in her 1969 book *On Death and Dying* developed a model for understanding the process that people go through as they come to terms with impending death. This modern classic of clinical psychology suggests that terminally ill patients pass through five stages as they learning to cope with the inevitable:

Stage 1: Denial and Isolation

Stage 2: Anger

Stage 3: Bargaining

Stage 4: Depression

Stage 5: Acceptance

The point behind the work is that different communication strategies are appropriate at each stage and that it is contingent on the doctors and nurses to use huge sensitivity and skill to move the patient as easily as possible towards Acceptance.

Kubler-Ross' work has been seized upon by change writers who draw parallels, not unnaturally, between death and organizational change. Philip G

Daryl R. Conner, 'the undisputed guru of the change management movement' is the founder and CEO of ODR Inc., a research and development firm. Now considered one of the leading authorities on the subject of organizational change, he has taken his learning to the boardrooms of such giants as Mobil Oil, JC Penney, Pepsi-Cola, Levi-Strauss and AT&T and consulted to organizations and governments in Europe, Latin America, Asia and the former Soviet Union. The list of other major consultancies who have woven his work into their own is impressive – IBM, McKinsey, Ernst & Young – and one of the surest signs that he must be onto something good.

His stance is to demystify the uncertainties of the human change with clear processes and vivid concepts. Chief of these is what Conner terms 'human resilience', which he says is what sets winners apart from those who are constantly feeling shattered by the increasing pace of discontinuous change. The five basic characteristics of resilient people are that they:

- display a sense of security and self-assurance that is based on their view of life as complex but filled with opportunity (**Positive**)
- have a clear vision of what they want to achieve (**Focused**)
- demonstrate a special pliability when responding to uncertainty (**Flexible**)
- develop structured approaches to managing ambiguity (**Organized**)
- engage change rather than defend against it (**Proactive**).

A strong picture of a resilient person is built up: someone who can expect paradoxes and uncertainty yet believes that even adversity is a teacher; someone who maintains the perspective given to them by a strong sense of purpose; someone who can display patience, humor and understanding when stress amongst others is high; someone who can shift their own frames of reference as the times demand; someone who looks for the common themes beneath myriad changes and applies thought and planning; someone who is happy to take risks and is good at getting the best out of the problem solving skills of the whole team. That's an impressive list of credentials, and I'd suggest that more people can display them than many change writers would have you believe. But how many individuals compose their CVs to demonstrate these strengths? How many companies have a recruitment process designed to spot them? We still live in an age when we hire for skills and train for attitude. We employ, train and reward people for their ability to fit into a particular, specialist box and are then surprised when they have difficulty either accommodating or moving out of that box.

The shift seems to be to hire for attitude first and, where necessary, train to enhance skills. (Southwest Airlines, the most profitable airline in history, suggest this as being the lynch pin of their hugely successful, people-oriented culture. Read *Nuts! Southwest Airline's Crazy Recipe for Business and Personal Success* by Kevin & Jackie Freiberg, Broadway Books 1997). Intuitively, you feel that's a good principle. I know many an IT Director, for example, who would happily trade a half-dozen of his programming geniuses for a couple of Conner's resilient people.

Clampitt in his excellent book *Communicating for Managerial Effectiveness* (Sage Publications 1991) provides a table that details how (and how not) to respond to the emotional and behavioral cues that indicate where your colleagues are in the process towards Acceptance.

Stage	Identifying actions	Appropriate actions	Inappropriate response
Denial	Not showing up for meetings	Discern actual points of resistance	Ignore the resistance
	Overly busy with routine tasks	Discuss positives and negatives of change	Ridicule the person's denial
	Less socializing	Legitimize concerns	
	Procrastinating	Discuss (sell) rationale of the change	

Stage	Identifying actions	Appropriate actions	Inappropriate response
Anger	Being irritable	Stay calm	Escalate into a relationship conflict
	Contemplating sabotage	Clarify the details of the change	threats
	Being confrontative	Show understanding of the anger whilst firmly emphasizing the need for change	Blame others for the change
	Appearing 'short-fused'		Take anger personally
		Allow some ventilation	
Bargaining	Trying to make deals	Be flexible with regard to inconsequential items	Reject suggestions briskly
	Trading favors		Give in to employee demands
	Promise making	Be firm with regard to the basic position	Give impression of agreement
		Focus on long-term benefits	
Depression	Being untalkative	Show concern	Pressurize for full acceptance
	Seeming apathetic	Give them space	Jest about feelings
	Missing work	Encourage discussions with others who have fully accepted change	Overly happy and giddy
	Appearing listless		
	Looking sombre		
Acceptance	Change is carefully implemented	Encourage auxiliary suggestions	'I told you so'
	Return to normal atmosphere	Resume 'normal' communication	Joke about previous reactions
		Praise	

Smart quotes

How to communicate change by anticipating resistance

Two of the provocative statements I've made in this book are

1. *People do not fear change*

and

2. People do not resist change.

I'll make another now:

3. People are naturally and effortlessly creative.

The statements are all linked. It is because they are naturally and effortlessly creative that people exhibit the behaviors which other people group together as 'resistance to change'. And these behaviors are a reaction not to the change, but to the way that the change is communicated.

For example:

- asking a naturally creative person *not* to help create a solution is an insult to their self-esteem

- asking a naturally creative person to accept a predetermined design or heavily-detailed and articulated plan is an insult to their self-respect.

So people may often sulk, or get depressed, because they feel they've been insulted. It may not be very mature or 'professional' behavior but let's be clear: they're not resisting the change, they're resisting you. They are showing you, in largely unconscious ways (because they'd probably not be brave enough to tell you this direct), that you have been rude, that you have been inconsiderate and that you have not been sufficiently audience-oriented in your communication.

A checklist for communicating change that puts people first

How will I:

- anticipate possible 'resistance' behavior by putting myself in their shoes and empathizing with their fears?

- show how the change is advantageous over past practices in ways that they themselves can empathize with?

- show how the change is about creating a better company for its stakeholders, and not an excuse for some consultant or the CEO to take an ego trip?

- demonstrate respect for the past practices, and not make my audience out to be wrong or stupid?

- show how soon and in what ways the benefits of the change will be observable by them?

- make it clear what the change is *not*?

- make it clear how I know that my audience have the capability to change and that this will always carry them through any problems or barriers that crop up.

- show that the change is clearly linked to the strategic direction of the organization or that it responds to some major shift in customer needs? In this way, I'll be able to show that the change is critical to the work of the company, and not something to 'get in the way' of that work.

- enlist their help in putting the detail onto the 'skeleton' of my change plan? What schedule of activities do I have planned that draws on their creativity (and not just their inclusion)?

- (sorry, you missed that, I must have been mumbling. I repeat:) What schedule of activities do I have planned that draws on their creativity (and not just their inclusion)?

- demonstrate that flexibility exists for altering the change program if it doesn't develop as hoped?

- choose which communication channel to use and when?

- encourage feedback? I could, for example, prepare a FAQ sheet about this change to demonstrate that I've done some consideration of what questions they might have? But what else could I do?

- ensure that I am open to all feedback? What channels could I put in place to capture possibly sensitive, personal and even anonymous feedback?

- after I have started to receive feedback, how will I demonstrate that I am listening and responding? I could, for example, keep issuing a bulletin of 'current concerns', and attach my response to each one, e.g.:

  - I know there's been some concern about layoffs ...

  - I know that some of you are worried about the new team structures ...

- demonstrate that I am already behaving in a way that is congruent with the change (e.g. if I'm talking about innovation, I give one or two innovative ways to receive feedback; if I'm talking about quality, I prepare excellent-looking handouts, etc.)?

- consider my overall communication strategy as being like an advertising campaign for the change; knowing that if I can influence them to *want* the change, I won't have to try too hard to make them have to do it?

- ensure that I'm keeping up communication *momentum* which encourages, prods and guides people towards the changed world, without it turning into communication *repetition* that turns them off (see the 7x rule)?

- ensure that I make it clear I am not blind to the pain and difficulty that change often brings

- enable and coach others in spreading this communication across the company?

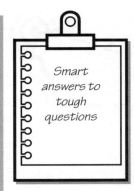
Q: OK so we've heard about resistance. But let's look on the positive side of things. How do I know my people are actually committed?

A: Conner suggests people pass through eight stages in demonstrating commitment. The first two are **Preparation** phase stages: first *contact* with the imminent change through a speech, memo, meeting conversation, then *awareness* that it will be happening. The next two stages are in the **Acceptance** phase are *understanding* and *positive perception*. The third and final phase, **Commitment**, where the change passes from the intentional to the actual, has four further stages. *Installation* is where the change is tested during a pilot period; *adoption* – where the test is rolled out more generally and over an extended duration; *institutionalization* – where systems and processes are redesigned to keep the change locked in and finally *internalization* – where the people affected have taken the change into their hearts, 'agreeing wholeheartedly' with it you might say.

- enable those others to deal with conflict that may arise (knowing that people might find 'the messengers' an easier target than me)?

I'd leave this chapter with a question.

The biggest problem with seeing change as goal-oriented is that momentum is built towards achieving that goal. All those project plans stack up,

'Five frogs sat on a log. One decided to jump. How many frogs are left?

'Five. There's a big difference between deciding to jump and actually jumping. Inspired leaders know how to get total commitment, so that no frogs are left on the corporate log. Zero-frog leadership.'

Gay Hendricks The Corporate Mystic

KILLER
QUESTIONS

I like this plan. Great. Now, what *do we do* if we get to point where the plan says we are ready to implement but we know that the majority of people are not truly committed? Will you sanction a delay in implementation, or will we go ahead regardless?

all with critical lines pointing towards the ultimate outcome. Businesses don't like to admit failure. 'We've set a goal and we will reach it; the project manager says that we will.'

The trouble is that people don't fit very well onto project plans. People change at different rates, for different reasons. Even after all your efforts to build consensus and trust, people may remain fickle and contrary. You are faced with a tough question: What happens if commitment level is at odds with the project plan?

7

Aligning the Organization: Part 3

CHANGING THE CULTURE

Organizations are like petri dishes. They breed cultures.

Ten smart things to know about corporate culture

1. We all create culture 100%. Even cynicism and apathy contributes to and is a real part of the culture that exists. Being smart is knowing that you have a choice of how to behave and that the choice creates the reality of your culture.

2. Just as the Spiral Pyramid model tells us we cannot not communicate, so with culture, we cannot not create it.

3. Some choose to tolerate, sustain or reproduce extrapolations of past cultures rather than create new ones, but in its way, that's still creation.

4. It's true that some cultures are shaped by strong leaders. But all that means is that they have greater powers of manifestation and focus – they set themselves way over on the side of creation rather than toleration.

5. Except in a very few, extraordinary cases, cultures suppress performance because they pull people back towards a past world (see diagram on p. 129). Except in a few, extraordinary cases, this expression of culture in the behavior of people is not wilful or malicious. If you are trying to pull your company towards the new value of *customer first* and everyone else seems stuck in the old value of *technology is King*, then they are unlikely to be doing that just to spite you. Rather they are acting in alignment with their own logic: *technology is King brings success, technology is King brings success, technology is King brings success*. Imagine their confusion when you tell them that *technology is King* is now insufficient. Tending to the confusion rather than punishing the resistance is a healthier way forward.

6. Remember that in culture change work, you're shifting not just your company's culture but a universal culture too.

Most cultures which now appear to hinder and suppress people are simply outcomes of a previous Age of Organizations. Almost since their inception, organizations have been designed to create order, to control diversity and surprise and to institutionalize behavior. And people at work adapted to that reality: business produced a 'culture of the workplace' that for many years was true for nearly all companies (and individual corporate cultures merely variations of this): *conform, don't rock the boat, follow the rules, peace brings pay* etc. We must remember that we live in a generation that has been born out of the

'Improvement require leadership. There can never be too much improvement. There can never be too much leadership. We must all be leaders and we must all be followers.'

Richard Koch

Note: there's another reason that Richard Koch is right to say we must all be leaders, in the classic sense of spotting opportunities and threats and shaking up the status quo to make things change. It is because of the old problem that every organization faces: that it is being led and directed by executives who are near to the end of their careers. Why on earth would they want to usher in transformation? They've only just got what they've worked for all their careers. What about the stock options? What about their pension? The irony is not just that the hungriest people are not in positions of political power; it is that their available role models may well be actively maintaining the status quo.

Smart quotes

HOW CULTURES THAT SUPPRESS PERFORMANCE AND CHANGE ARE FORMED

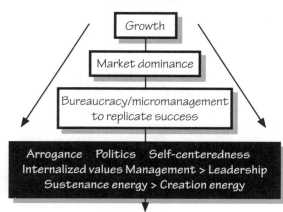

Growth

Market dominance

Bureaucracy/micromanagement to replicate success

Arrogance   Politics   Self-centeredness
Internalized values Management > Leadership
Sustenance energy > Creation energy

old 'culture of the workplace' – my father lived that culture and yours probably did too.

Only recently have we decided to design organizations that release potential, maximize creativity and nurture knowledge. Changing our beliefs about what we want our organizations to do takes seconds. Shifting the organizational structure and systems to reflect and align with our belief takes much longer. How long does it take for a society to develop a new 'culture of the workplace' which matches these new organizations? Years. A generation? And people will react to the liberation implied by a new 'culture of the workplace' at vastly differing rates and with different degrees of openness.

7. *Culture is learned and transmissible.*

As individuals we are, ultimately, mutable entities who can be moulded by the culture into which we are introduced. People create their environments and are shaped by them. That's why much of change is about *unlearning* the old way of doing things

8. *Culture is a dynamic system that changes continuously over time.*

This means that the learning is never finished. In other words, the capacity to learn is innate in a culture unless artificial controls are imposed to the contrary. (In the movie *Jurassic Park*, the most frightening thing about the chief horror creatures, the Velociraptors, was their ability to learn, which moved them one huge evolutionary step closer to us). The fact that cultures do change should give us comfort when we are contemplating trying to change them.

9. *Culture is selective.*

Culture implies choices – all cultures are made up of a series of selections from the whole of possible human behavior and experience. It is the choices that the group has made, consciously and unconsciously, that identify it as having its own culture and that separate it from other groups which have made different choices. In the UK, for example, we have selected individualism. Japan has selected communalism. The US teaches the value of youth, in China one learns to respect and treasure the elderly. In Japan work is selected as an end, in the UK it is learned as a means. There's nothing genetic which tells a Japanese child that work is an end in itself. She learns that it has been chosen as appropriate by her society and adapts accordingly. This cultural resonance communicates into products and work values and must be taken into account.

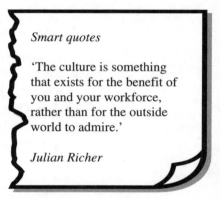

Smart quotes

'The culture is something that exists for the benefit of you and your workforce, rather than for the outside world to admire.'

Julian Richer

10. *Culture is septocentric.*

From the Latin: *septum*, 'partition.' Cultures are inherently separatist. We always perceive cultures from our own position at the centre of one. This is why organizations find it so hard to conceive of learning a different way of doing things ('it would never work like that around here!'). This is a peculiar defence mechanism whereby people complain about their corporate culture in one breath and claim it's impossible to change it in the next.

The simplicity of culture change: working with what works

The key to culture change is very, very straightforward. Since culture is what you create whether you intend to or not, it means that you're creating it (or sustaining/reproducing it) every minute of the day. You are already making culture. Everything you think you need to change culture you already have. Everything you think you need to learn you already know. Exactly the same principles that you follow to create a great culture you are already following to create your awful one. So the simplicity of culture change is in changing how individuals think and act. Remember:

1. Knowing what you want above all else creates culture

Your company may well prove this point perfectly already. The problem in most companies is that they haven't really sorted out what their vision is, what they want above all else. As a result, their culture is fragmented or unclear. Or perhaps most companies secretly want a 'great culture' about third on the list after strong profits and increasing revenues. So they produce a culture which is a reflection of that position on the need-hierarchy.

This is why it is crucial to co-create a vision, gain commitment to it and so on – but also ask yourself if you *really* want it. Are you prepared for the implications of what you say you want?

I've seen companies publish vision statements which attest to the faith they have in the talent of their people, when they clearly haven't come to terms with what that faith might mean for them as leaders. Really, in their heart of hearts, they are not ready to trust, empower and develop their people. Really, in their heart of hearts, they still want to control them. And corporate cultures are born out of what the leaders really, really want, not what they really, really say.

2. Aligning everything behind your vision creates culture

And your company probably proves this too. But if vision is unclear, then

At Mitel Corp of Canada, people in the testing department routinely dupli-cated tests already performed by their colleagues in the design and engi-neering departments. We now have a 'one test' policy that has shaved an entire week off the average product-development time.

Change is part of the culture now. The attitude is, if your see something that doesn't make sense, get rid of it. People simply don't stand for roadblocks any more.

Stephen Quesnelle, Head of Quality Programs

alignment is going to be imperfect. Perhaps, your company want lots of different things above all else, and aligns various systems and processes variously with those wants. Fragmented wants are reflected in fragmented systems to reinforce a fragmented culture. Or perhaps they still have sys-tems which are a hangover from old ways of doing things. So for example, the management exhortation is towards risk taking and innovation, but the sign-off procedure for getting the necessary budget is slow, bureau-cratic and untrusting. Or the value is towards team work, but the reward system is geared towards individual achievement.

Culture change is not a black art, is not a mystery. It doesn't even matter what definition of culture you use, or what dimensions you think it has. Who cares what I define as culture? Or Charles Handy? Use whatever definition works for you. And decide what its chief components are in your company.

All that matters is that for each area of culture you've identified as weak, you create a new awareness of what you have and what you want, and then align your behaviors and systems around that.

HOW MISALIGNMENT UNDERMINES VISION IN SEVEN AREAS OF CULTURE

Cultural dimension 1: climate

Vision	*Reality*
'a fun environment'	gossip-ridden; moods are left to fester; unrelieved busy-ness

Cultural dimension 2: focus

Vision	*Reality*
'a strong sense of purpose'	direction limited and/or unstated; not broken into specific strategies or team objectives

Cultural dimension 3: leadership & management

Vision	*Reality*
'empowering role models'	managers hoard information; inter-competitive

Cultural dimension 4: structure, systems

Vision	*Reality*
'fast decision-making'	bureaucratic checks and permission-gaining systems

Cultural dimension 5: resources

Vision	*Reality*
'experts with complimentary skills'	under-utilized skills

Cultural dimension 6: personal development

Vision	*Reality*
'grow great people'	appraisal system backwards looking; 'no time' for training

In other words:

Awareness

- know what you want

- know where you are.

Alignment

- change your behaviors, your systems and your attitudes
  until they are in alignment with what you want

- maintain awareness to help track your progress

- work with what works; learn from and discard what doesn't.

> **Smart things to say about change**
>
> The most powerful lever in culture change is sincerely *wanting* to change. The measure of our success in all this will be how much we really want things to be different.

Even as a smart change leader, you'd be surprised how many people who spend 50 hours or more of their lives in a toxic culture really want it to be different (they're not masochists, you know). You'd be surprised how much energy is released when you involve people in creating a new purpose.

The next most powerful levers are the symbolic and the heroic – things people see and the labels they put on that. That's why if you can't change the people, you must change the people, i.e. ask them to leave. As long as it's not just done as a power kick, sweeping out 'the old guard' who created the old, inappropriate-to-now culture, can accelerate culture change dramatically.

EIGHT EXAMPLES OF POSITIVE ALIGNMENT INTERVENTIONS

- *Job description*
  every position from post room assistant to CEO has a mandate and an expectation that they will create change, challenge the status quo, work in context of the vision.
- *Leadership*
  models and influences and reinforces employee acceptance and understanding of the new culture at every opportunity – *what* and *why*.
- *Performance measurement*
  ensures that it rewards results derived from application of new values and beliefs.
- *Recruitment*
  from advertisement to job offer letter, the process emphasizes 'fit' with the new culture.
- *Communication*
  every email sent has a signature file with a quotation chosen to reflect the new values or purpose.
- *Training*
  suppliers chosen primarily on their understanding of the change, and for their capacity to adapt their material to the new culture, both in content and style.
- *Customer*
  PR, advertising and corporate literature presents and the new culture and explains how it will enhance both product and service.
- *Office design*
  enables the behaviors implied by the vision; is fresh, clean, bright.

At the same time, it's possible to enhance the new values and norms of culture by promoting those who exhibit the Vision in their behaviors. Even better, break the rules to make a positive example of them – promote outside traditional promotion times, or outside the traditional parameters of career advancement.

But cultures cannot just be illustrated – they must be explained, too, otherwise they are open to misinterpretation. The leader must say, in effect, these are *what* the new cultural norms are – this is how things are going to be done around here – and this is *why* ...

It is this combination of information and experience which will help patterns of belief to shift. This in turn will feed into the communication network and will generate a new set of shared assumptions and values which are the grounding of the new culture. Culture change is about provoking and sustaining new norms.

Aligning the culture behind your vision allows change to flow easily through the organization. Misalignment causes confusion and conflict to arise.

8

Aligning the Organization: Part 4

MEASURING AND EVALUATING THE IMPACT OF CHANGE INITIATIVES

'Not everything that can be counted counts, and not everything that counts can be counted.'

Albert Einstein

This chapter is about agreeing the benefits and measures of change projects. And it is about reviewing regularly to check that you are on target.

In other words it is about:

Awareness

- know what you want

- know where you are.

Alignment

- change your behaviors, your systems and your attitudes until they are in alignment with what you want

- maintain awareness of what is happening around you so that you can continuously adjust your behavior

- work with what works; learn from and discard what doesn't

Change wants proof

Change can be a doubting Thomas. It needs signs and assurances. It does not hold much truck with words alone, no matter who the speaker might be. 'I'm back!' announces Christ, claiming a transformation of some substantial power and depth. 'Yeah, yeah, back, schmack!' says Thomas, 'Prove

SMART VOICES

We sweated blood and tears to create and implement the system that they'd requested. It was one all-nighter after the other. Pepsi by the case. Cold pizza for breakfast. Non-stop work. And it felt great. In fact, we had a better team spirit on that project than at any time since our division was created. The trouble was, next time we put our heads above water, we realized the department we were producing the system for had ceased to exist. We were just 'making it happen'. We got sucked into that old macho thing that if you're sweating, panting and have calluses on your hands, then you must be doing a good job.

Systems analyst, High Street Bank

it! Show me the wound in your side. Oh! OK, well it looks real enough ...
But I bet I can't put my fingers all the way ... Oh. Urrrgh! Jesus!!! Christ!
It is you!!'

- Change demands real, measurable, undeniable, agreed-in-advance proof.

- It also needs regular checks along the way that things are moving in the
  required direction.

Now we know that working hard needs to coincide with working smart.

When you're proposing change you need to demonstrate that you are thinking in solid terms about visible and concrete changes to the way the organization works, rather than noble but vague hopes of something better
than now.

Showing that you are prepared and able to measure and evaluate change:

- is probably the *only* way you'll get any funding or resources for the
  change effort

- shows that there is a left brain rigor and discipline to change, even though
  (as this book has shown) the real work of change is in the softer, psychological areas of human experience

- gets them emotionally involved in the change, because you'll be showing how the change helps them

- helps to gain commitment since your measures will be telling them what
  benefits they'll be able to see and when

Q: 'Oh come on, making things happen is what it's all about. You can spend all
   the time you want fantasizing. But in this company, we still measure by
   results! When are we going to stop thinking about the future and get on
   with it?
A: 'I understand your frustration. I just want to ensure we're getting the results we really want. I want to help prevent us climbing up ladders only to
   find we've been leaning them against the wrong walls.'

- keeps people on side during times of change fatigue, stress and disillusionment since you'll be able to demonstrate the signposts you have
passed and those that are coming up next. In other words, it breaks
down long and complex changes into definite stages or sections.

What proof is like

Change challenges you: 'Prove it'

- You wanted to write poetry? Prove it – show me.

- You wanted to go the gym three times a week? Prove it – show me.

- You wanted to improve communication with your spouse? Prove it –
show me.

- You wanted to beta test the Thorax Module and have it implemented
by Easter? Prove it – show me.

- You wanted to create a culture of innovation and intelligent risk-tak-
ing? Prove it – show me.

SO, YOU WANTED BETTER COMMUNICATION IN YOUR TEAM?

Just some signs of change to prepare for

- **Visual** – things look different.
  People who didn't sit together at lunch. There are more ad hoc meetings between team members. The flow of emails between people has changed (e.g. people 'cc'd' where necessary that weren't 'cc'd' before). There's a statement of purpose to look at. There's a newsletter. There's an event set up in your Organizer for next month inviting users to come and meet the team and market progress on your project work. Members smile more and frown less.
- **Aural** – things sound different.
  The ratio between people asking questions and making statements changes. People use more collaborative, inquiring, sensitive, congratulatory language. There is more silence than there was in meetings, because people are actually listening and/or reflecting. There is more noise than there was in meetings because people are contributing, challenging, laughing.
- **Numerical** – things take less or more time to count.
  The number of emails on team-related matters increases (this includes emails propagating the social glue – jokes, invitations to the bar, etc.).
- **Feeling** – things feel different.
  You feel that the statement of purpose is both relevant and is being acted upon. You feel that the laughter is genuine rather than forced. You feel a sense of truth and honesty in conversations with your team members. You feel you are making realistic progress towards the goal of 'better communication'. In this example, feeling things have changed is an extra verification of the visual, aural and numerical ones. If the numbers tell you that change has happened, but you don't feel that it has, you might want to ask other questions. Am I actually measuring the right things? What measures have I missed?

So how can you prove the change you're working on is happening?

If you're changing your clothes, you can tell when it's happened. Some clothes that you didn't have on a few minutes ago are reflected back at you in the mirror. Your old ones lie crumpled on the floor or gather creases on the end of the bed. *Your evidence is visual.*

If you're changing your address after a house move, you can tell (usually) when you have typed out your new details on a postcard and mailed them off to your friends. You can tell the change has been successful because you still receive Christmas cards and the phone still rings occasionally. *Your evidence is visual and aural.*

If you decide to change your income for the better, you can tell you've been successful because the number on the bottom line of your bank account is bigger than it used to be and is printed in black rather than red. *Your evidence is numerical.*

Any change, no matter how 'woolly' or banal, produces outward, observable, concrete signs.

It is no different in your change project.

How do you show/prove that your change is working? You agree and design the benefits and measures into your change plan *before* you start.

Gaining commitment by agreeing shared benefits and measures

The measures that will prove that the change is real need to grow naturally out of the questions which drive the change in the first place. Although measures appear to be the end point, you need to plan for them from the beginning.

1. Ask yourself: what's in it for me?

- Clarify why you personally want the change – career consideration, skills development, experience, to get noticed, to help a colleague?

- Separate out your business result (cost reduction, process redesigned, revenue increased etc.) and personal win (status, prestige, fame, self-esteem, increased skill or competence)?

- How will *you* know when you've succeeded in each of these areas? Is that realistic? Are you a good personal judge of your own work in life? Are you too easy or hard on yourself?

Note: The accepted wisdom in change is to say that it doesn't really matter what you do unless you get external verification of your actions. The customer counts. Our model of communication (see Chapter 6) certainly agrees that the audience is the ultimate arbiter of 'success'.

The trouble with that model is that it doesn't have any sympathy for the disparity of effort. All-powerful as your audience or customer is, it won't actually be them pulling another all-nighter, and eating stale pizza with hygienically challenged colleagues at 3.30 a.m. They won't be having a dark night of the soul three months hence when morale seems to be down, cost seems to be up and the project's one leap from disaster. They'll just swan in every so often and say 'Yup' or 'No way'. And on that judgment, your achievement will rest. This is why it is crucial that any project begins with your relationship to it. How much do *you* want the change? How serious are you about making the change – and living with it? How deeply can you understand what this change might bring you, so that you can create for yourself a whole raft of motivations and reassurance that will take you through good and bad times? What are the benefits you expect as change leader?

2. Ask your main stakeholders (change customer, change leader or sponsor, team members, suppliers): what's in it for them?

- Who will be involved?

- What role will they play?

- Clarify what the change implies for them.

- Agree on why you want the change: what are the benefits for other stakeholders?

  - what are their business results and personal wins?

  - are the benefits *at least* as powerful for them as for you?

- How can you enlist their aid?

- Who will else it impact? What changes elsewhere in the system can you predict?

- What are the anticipated benefits? Are they attractive enough to pull you (all) forward, even when things get tough?

- What are the anticipated costs? Money, people, time, impact on other projects, personal time away from family? Are they too much pain for you (all) to bear now? If you're brave enough to set off regardless, do you anticipate a lean time ahead? What about when things get tougher? How painful do those costs feel then?

- What are their main priorities at the moment and what are they anticipating might crop up in the near future and disable your project?

- How can you manage that?

- What skills or knowledge could they contribute to helping this project succeed?

- What skills or knowledge do we need to bring in from outside?

Note: If the benefits from this change aren't clear and attractive to your stakeholders, you lose. If your customers don't want it at least as badly as you, they won't give you the necessary patience or fair and honest feedback you'll require. You'll also lack committed project leaders, sponsors or champions.

If your colleagues (peers or bosses) in the company don't understand how important/urgent your change is, they won't free up more resources to share with you when you need them. Another significant danger in getting their benefits and yours out of balance (i.e. they should be roughly equal for all parties or over-weighted in their favor) is that you'll lose the ability to make them responsible and accountable for the change. After all, if you're project is going to change the working practices in a colleague's department in a way that brings it in line with the corporate push towards 'customer first', your colleague will need to own the change in receiving it as much as you do in giving it.

If your team members don't understand and want the change at both a personal and business level, they won't feel like drawing on their personal reserves of energy when the going gets rough (as it will). They won't feel able to phone home and tell their kids that they'll miss putting them to bed again tonight.

3. Agree a shared understanding of the measures for success

(i) Use the conscious brain

Collate all the personal wins and business benefits generated from the questions above.

Ask: what obviously has to happen for all stakeholders to call this successful – in other words what is this project's definition of the word 'success'?

Note: The advertising campaign has to be delivered on time and within budget. Easy. But what else has to happen to convince people that it's a success? Positive customer feedback? Heavy editorial press coverage and comment (and how many column inches constitutes heavy)? Increased sales? If these indicators are not within the scope of your project, you have to work overtime to persuade people to share your understanding that they aren't. You could break corporate records for keeping project costs down – but if your stakeholders were expecting increased press coverage too, they wouldn't thank you for your work. They'd judge you a failure.

(ii) Use your sub-conscious brain
Here's an exercise.

Take some moments to relax and visualize the change as successful. Pack as much detail as you can into your visualization – take care over building the physical environment in your vision. What do your colleagues wear in your envisioned meetings? What is there tone of voice when they speak? Visit other stakeholders in your dream. Ask them how they know the project has been a success – what is happening now in that changed world to show that the change is happening:

- what quantifiable/objective measures might there be in place if you were to walk up to someone in your vision and say 'Prove it' (visual, aural, numerical)

- what subjective measures are there – what feelings does your vision generate in you?

Come out of your vision and write down any new measures it generated.

(iii) Select from (i) and (ii) the key measures of success
Note: Make sure you are not pressurizing yourself to 'think corporate'

and make your measures purely financial. All you have to worry about is making the measures measurable.

A measure is measurable if:

- you can independently and objectively assess a change in visual, aural, behavioral and numerical parameters

- you can clearly answer either yes or no to straightforward questions about the change.

4. Agree some intermediate measures

- moving-towards signs – i.e. things that you would see and hear happening that would assure you you were on the way to the benefit

- moving-away signs – i.e. things that you would see and hear happening that would assure you that you were moving away from the benefit.

You have to know that you are on the right path, since in any major change, the final destination may be some way off. You can't wait until to get to the coast before you reflect on your surroundings and say 'Yup, this is Brighton.'

5. Write a change compact, version 1

Draw up a document that, for each stakeholder, details the role they will play in the project, the intended benefits of the change for them and the measure and definitions of success they expect to be able to see, hear, count or otherwise gauge. Also include a list of milestones with dates as intermediate measures.

This document will eventually be signed and dated by all parties as a commitment to change.

6. *Write your project plan and adjust your compact document if necessary*

Draw up your plan: how, by whom and when etc.

- Do you need to make any adjustments to the benefits and measures listed in the compact, now that your project has taken a major step towards reality?

- In particular, do you need to recalibrate the anticipated project cost?

7. *Publish and agree the compact of project benefits, measures and milestones*

- Seek feedback. Negotiate meanings. Produce and publish a 'final' agreed compact.

- Hold a formal yet fun event to mark the signing of the compact.

- Use the compact not only for review against progress but also as the basis or skeleton of any marketing efforts you might make on this project's behalf in the future.

8. *Set up the organizational scanners to spot the signposts up as they happen*

Be aware yourself
Pay double attention – focus at the level of what's happening and what

might happen; what's happened and what hasn't; what's said and what's left unsaid.

Enlist help
Coach people to realize that their job is not just about making the change happen, it's about being observers and witnesses of it. It's their job to join in the Question stage so that they can own both the problem and the need for change. It's their job to Theorize and push themselves and the project beyond the humdrum and comfortable. It's their job to take Courageous Action. And it's their job to Reflect honestly and candidly about the project's success. In total it is everyone's job to make sure we are in Alignment with our Vision. No prizes here for stepping out of the wreckage of a failed project and saying: 'I knew that would happen!'

Open up
Hold formal reviews – by carrying out stakeholder research. These audits can be carried out by insiders. They will only be as objective as the auditors' maturity and self-awareness, but what you might lose in objectivity you will gain in marketing benefits ('we are demonstrating that we're not afraid of feedback'). If you're deadly serious about objectivity, get an outsider in.

Hold semi-formal reviews – at team meetings. Ask:

- what's happening to take us towards the goal?

- what's happened last week that failed to move us forward, or took us down old paths that we agreed we wanted to change?

- what specifically can each of us we do next week that will move us towards our goal?

Q: How much time should we spend 'reflecting' on results?

A: The usual answer is 'as much time as we can spare until it gets in the way of the real work'. That's why learning doesn't happen but lots of uninformed action does.

My answer is: as often as you sense it is helping. As much as learning demands it.

You should communicate about results, to people inside and outside the project, probably a little more than they'd tell you they'd want it, but not so much that it pisses them off. The criterion question is: does this communication aid the audience and does it aid the result of the project?

Clearly you need to formally review changes after the project has officially ended, and at regular periods after it (e.g. every six months) to confirm that the change is continuing in place rather than regressing. These formal reflections have a tendency to focus on the most obvious and significant changes. That's why they are often called 'reviews' – it has that sense of 'assessing performance'.

But you need to be reflecting on as well as measuring it, so that you're learning as much as you are moving. Discussing progress towards the results checks that your ladder is leaning against the wall you'd hoped, and that it is leaning there without causing any majorly unanticipated pain. If the environment has changed sufficiently that the benefits are no longer going to be relevant, then that will set you off on another learning cycle, the Action stage of which might be as profound as cancelling the project. How you cancel a project without losing face is a change challenge as meaningful as any in this book.

Talking about progress has other benefits than just that showing if project's working against plan or not. It maintains a focus on learning. It keeps the vision current. It convinces people that everyone's still serious about making this change happen, since anything the company spends its time on (and this is as true for reflecting as it is for action) is an indicator of importance. Use it well. Ask not just what has happened? or what might happen next? Also ask: what does that/will that mean for us?

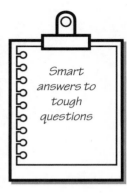

Smart answers to tough questions

Hold informal reviews – manage by walking about. Ask 'How's it going? Great? Can you show me what you're up to at the moment? Show me any problems you've got presently.'

Most of all, talking about progress throws up an opportunity to react to unanticipated benefits. Your project is a learning project as much as a change project. You team will change as they work as they learn. They will increase their knowledge and they will heighten their awareness. So much of their competence and values and sense of esteem will (under your leadership) be exercised as they work that they cannot help but grow as human beings. They'll naturally become Curious and ask smarter Questions. They'll come up with more Creative Theories. They'll be braver and more Courageous in suggesting and taking Action. They'll Reflect more deeply. One of the results of this is that they'll spot things happening that others don't, and that you certainly didn't anticipate when you wrote the plan. They'll see the environment around the project shift, and they'll draw creative links to those changes, tying possible new benefits into the scope of this project.

KILLER
QUESTIONS

REVIEWING FOR LEARNING AND PROGRESS

At each review stage, Reflect:

- 'Are we on target?'
- 'What are we learning about this project?'
- 'What are we learning for the future?'
- 'How is this project and its team changed since the last review?'
- 'How are our stakeholders changing?'
- 'How is the environment changing?'
- 'How do we feel?'
- '... and what does all that mean for us?'

Of course:

- You will need to take each of these new benefits through a process of signal setting and measurement as the ones you had anticipated.

- You will need to make a judgment as to whether each of these associated benefits is, realistically, a part of your project, or worthy of a completely new one.

So review. But don't just measure. Talk. Learn. *Reflect.*

Soft measures are hard

Hard measures are those financial, bottom-line impacts that no company can do without. They are how operational performance has traditionally been assessed, and is still the main information in Annual Statements. If you increase revenue, that's a hard measure. Reducing the cycle time of your product to inception to market is another. Reducing the time it takes to fulfil a customer lead, that's another. These hard measures are also known as Key Performances Indicators (KPIs).

Anybody who tells you that hard measures are all that matters should be sent to see the corporate physician.

Soft measures are all those things which a company also depends on which business has traditionally tried to keep a distance from because they present new challenges to the number crunchers. How has customer perception changed? How wide and deep is this company's knowledge in its chosen areas of speciality? How innovative are we? How happy/proud/ committed to this company is its work force?

These and measures like them are critical (perhaps we should replace KPI with the more inclusive CSF – Critical Success Factors). They are the discomforting questions that produce (should produce) the hard measures we're worshipped for so long (whereas improving hard measures doesn't guarantee improved soft ones). The old saw: 'what gets measured gets managed' is now in danger of becoming true in a way it never really was before. In reality, 'cycle time' is never managed. People behaving in innovative and collaborative ways that result in reduced cycle times, that's what's managed.

Part of the problem that you'll encounter in the hard/soft debate is that the very word 'measure' has mechanical, numerical associations which are very powerful and speak attractively to the left brain, analytical dominance of much of management. Numerical measurement alone has a tendency to produce feelings of superiority, doubt or competition – not all of which are healthy human values. The man who measures his penis with a ruler is more likely to refer to a chart for comparison and worry, than decide what he can do to change his sexual performance so that the measurement matters less. But the word 'measure' has other meanings. By choosing the word for the title of his play *Measure for Measure*, Shakespeare was indicating 'fairness' and 'appropriateness'. Don't just count the indicators of performance. Question their appropriateness to the purpose of the work and of the company.

The other problem is that hard measures tend to be backwards-looking – records of what's happened. In your project, you can't afford not to be reflecting on what is happening and what might happen.

What *is* powerful about the sort of hard measures found in Annual Reports is that it is always comparative. 'These are 1998's figures; and here is 1999. What does the difference teach us?'

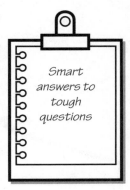
Q: What's the point of worrying so much about these hard and soft benefits?
A: If we don't, we'll never be able to comprehensively track our performance against strategic goals. Our corporate mission, for example, advertises that we'll be 'continuously improving'? It talks about how innovative we'll be. How can we tell these things just by looking at revenue and profit? Linking hard to soft measures also demonstrates that we're serious about these value statements – and that has a morale and customer-perception benefit too.

Your reflections and reviews should likewise produce meaning through relating one thing to another. What have we achieved? Where is that in relation to where we anticipated we'd be? What does that tell us? What new questions does that prompt us to ask?

Measuring the unmeasurable: chase your dreams down to specifics

Suppose you want the team to have higher morale. That is a soft goal, and at the moment it is too vague. How can you measure it? Ask: what would higher morale look like if it were there?

- fewer sick days?

- increased attendance at team meetings?

- increased involvement at team meetings?

- more effective handling of problems?

- *and what would that look like?*

- shorter time from problem identification to solution

- more positive language at problem identification ('can do' rather than blame or denial language).

All theses elements are measurable – providing you have the energy and patience to do so (and that is part of the change).

Ask your team for their ways of measuring higher morale. There might be a simple, creative way in there that you hadn't thought of.

These questions and enquiries create considered, shared and meaningful measurements.

Your next step is to ask, in each of these soft measures: 'What can I do today to help register a good score? What should I do tomorrow to make these benefits real? Why wait to measure them? What can I change *now*?'

KILLER QUESTIONS

OK: tell me: how far is the performance of this company driven by 'soft' issues, and how many on 'hard'?

9

Aligning the Organization: Part 5

THE PLAYERS – ROLES AND RESPONSIBILITIES DURING CHANGE

'It is requir'd you do awake your faith.'

Shakespeare, *The Winter's Tale*, V iii

Organizational change is multi-faceted. Organizations have responded to this reality by dividing the complexity into specific roles, each with its own particular responsibility. If we're all playing our assigned parts, the thinking goes, the whole thing should pretty much hang together.

The more traditional and linear the change project, the more likely the Smart Change Master is to be asked to play a particular role – leader, follower, sponsor, agent. In fact, reality is not as segmented as that, and you are likely to have to play different roles in different situations. It is perhaps as constructive to consider general groupings – or dimensions – of influence, as well as distinct roles.

There are three main dimensions.

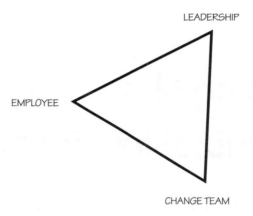

(i) Driving organizational change: the leadership dimension

The outside world, changing continuously as it is bound to do, throws up a myriad opportunities or threats. The role of leadership is to translate this need for change into a business case.

When the outside changes have presented themselves in a sufficiently un-avoidable way, the leader or leaders must first understand what is happening. Most of all they need to make a decision that change is necessary within the organization. The word decision derives from Latin words which mean *to cut off (from)*. Making a decision means that you are cutting yourself off – temporarily at least – from all other decisions that you might have made. A decision implies genuine, unmistakable certainty and commitment. Making a decision to change means that you are deadly serious about change.

Researchers tell us that roughly two-thirds of all change initiatives fail to deliver the expected benefits. Most post-mortems focus on poor communication, bad planning, or not shifting the cultural baseline to support the attempted process changes. I reckon the majority of changes fail because the original decision was not cut off from other possibilities, but was, rather, a fudge, a hope, a fingers-crossed prayer that things would turn out all right whilst we all carried on with business as usual. I can tell you what many leaders really, really want. And it's not change.

Indecision ripples out along the duration of a change program. Maybe that's what people resist.

At this stage, the leaders may take themselves off on a retreat to get themselves clear on the need for change. This may be seen as a jolly, and that is another of the silly myths organizations create. In fact, a retreat may be crucial to get the leadership clear and committed and working together. There's little point (though many try) in persuading the rest of the company that change is crucial, when the leadership don't understand or believe in the change themselves.

KILLER QUESTIONS

OK we're thinking about change. What does it take to make us *decide* to change?

Fragmentation ripples out along the duration of a change program. Maybe that's what people resist.

If you're thinking about change, are you clear yet on what you want?

Retreats should, if facilitated well, allow the top team to reflect on the underlying purpose of the company, without which no congruent Vision can flow. Retreats also allow leaders to face up to the reality of where the company is in the world, not in an environment of recrimination or fault-seeking, but in the sense of taking full responsibility for having made it so.

Another important thing happens on retreats like this. The top team bonds. They learn about each other, their individual and collective strengths and weaknesses. This allows them to assign key roles (who'll do the most communicating, who'll be in charge of the Plan) and anticipate threats that their weaknesses might create as the change program progresses.

From this new-found unity, the top team can draw up the first draft of the change strategy. This strategic direction will galvanize the company to action, first as a Vision of the desired future, communicated across the organization in a series of workshops or other formal events, then as a benchmark or reference point for future dilemmas that need to be resolved. Even better, perhaps part of their decision is to share the vision-making process with everyone in the company. One of the central themes of this book is that involvement is crucial to change projects – it helps people own the outcomes. There is no reason why this involvement cannot extend to sharing in the creation of the statement of corporate purpose and direction. (For ideas and strategies towards Shared Vision, see *The Fifth Discipline Handbook*, by Peter Senge and others – Nicholas Brealey 1996.)

From then on, leadership's role is primarily to model the values and behavior that the Vision implies. They need to demonstrate what it is they want. If the change is towards teamworking, they have to show that they are excellent team players themselves and that they have zero tolerance towards anti-team behaviors. If they want the organization to put customers first, they have to show examples of how they have done the same.

They need to oversee and champion the overall change design in the organization, using their political power always in favor of the original change decision. They need to know – and demonstrate that they know – that the change is on track. And they also need to leave themselves open to new information that may influence the program – a change in the environment that necessitates more speed, perhaps, or a slightly different emphasis.

Leadership stands tall. It expresses itself in grand, meaningful, symbolic gestures. It has the loudest voice, and where necessary, it can say, as no-one else can, 'Just do it – or else!'

The work of the leader is to:

- own and maintain the vision

- take ownership of the change benefits and ultimate responsibility for achieving them

- influence the organization as a whole to become aligned with the vision

- keep their pulse on the vitality of the change project and give whatever treatment is necessary

- communicate information verbally and electronically

- communicate meaning in their actions

- nurture relationships

- resolve conflict where it is damaging

- create conflict where there is complacency

- sell ownership and accountability

- promote self-responsibility

- agree a project scope, objectives and success criteria with the Change Team

- free-up funding, resources and staff

- review and approve progress and any deviations from the plan.

But leadership needs to be supported. Someone needs to do the real work.

(ii) Driving organizational change: the change team dimension

Talking about Vision and Strategic Direction and Purpose and how the planets have conspired to make the change Necessary has its downside. The trouble with being so high up is that you tend to get a bit isolated. And unabashed enthusiasm tires everyone, eventually.

The idea of a Change Team is that a group of people get together who share enough political power to make things happen and enough credibility at all levels of the company to gain acceptance and approval for the change.

Change teams need to be made up of a strong cross-section of the company. This is so they have immediate information gathering and sending channels open to the team all the way from director level to shop-floor or point-of-sale. They can easily listen to and feed the rumor network. The strong cross-section also allows all departments and disciplines in the organization to be represented, so that the implications of the change are understood everywhere.

It needs to be big enough that the ones who aren't in it can't easily block the change with bureaucratic fudge. So senior managers need to be part of the change team, not just willing youngsters.

But because the Change Team has so many potentially conflicting points of view, it has to learn to act as a team, sharing a common vision and having agreed principles for solving disagreement. Becoming a change team takes time – quite apart from all the time it will use up advocating and creating change. So one of the roles of leadership, we see, is giving the necessary permission for change team efforts to have precedence over other company concerns.

The work of the change team is to

- make sure it has the right amount and mix of members

- learn how to be a team (what is its purpose and objectives/how will it behave)

- understand the need for change, as passed on from the leadership

- help shape the vision and adapt its messages so that it can be communicated to all audiences in the company and using a variety of channels

- shake up the status quo

- identify exactly what the change is, who it targets and how it can be leveraged

- design the new work processes and culture

- align strategic and operational concerns

- derive specific goals from the Vision and oversee their achievement

- lead or champion change leadership courses

- organize change communication

- diagnose and solve problems and inhibitors to change as they arise

- maintain relentless momentum, learning and freshness

- encourage all managers or team leaders to propagate these objectives and behaviors

- be a source of mentorship and coaching.

The last two activities ensure that the spirit of leadership – which is essentially is about understanding and conveying the need for change – is cascaded throughout the organization.

Change teams are made up of change agents, which is a role you may be formally given in some organizations, but is most likely a status you acquire because of the qualities you exhibit.

Are you a change agent?

Tick the boxes which apply to you.

A change agent

☐ advocates change; speaks up against the status quo

☐ is highly future-oriented, always sees the future as different from the past

☐ likes to take new paths to reach uncharted territory

☐ is passionately convinced about what he or she does

☐ looks at change as an opportunity

☐ is part of a very influential minority

☐ does not get discouraged easily

☐ has a broad perspective, makes lots of connections

☐ listens very well; is listened to

☐ has the courage to guess and to trust his or her intuition

☐ has influence beyond his or her place in the organization; is not limited by position

☐ has little respect for status in its own right.

KILLER QUESTIONS

Are these the sorts of competencies we reward in our company? Really? I'm sorry. I thought we discouraged many of them. When did we stop doing that then?

(iii) Driving organizational change in the 'employee' dimension

Note: There is still no phrase to best describe those people in the change program who are neither leaders or change agents. Daryl Conner describes them as the 'targets'; yet isn't the true target of change the vision or objective? The people are the means to that end, the implementors of the change. At the same time, everyone is an implementor of change, from CEO to temp; this is especially true when we are advocating total involvement in the change process. One day there'll be a term to describe the role that these joint-participants in change play, without it appearing that they are hapless victims of someone else's mad plans.

For the time being I'll stick to the most rational – and therefore perhaps the coldest – term to describe everyone else who is not a leader, nor a change team member: *employee*.

By the way, this is not just a piece of authorial angst, nor an appeal for sympathy for the paucity of my imagination. If the key players in your change project are given fancy titles like leader or agent, how is that going to feel to those who are left with the bit parts? How are you going to guarantee the involvement and solidarity of those players who only get to put 'one of the crowd' on their CV? How will you bridge the us/them divide?

Reread Chapter 6, by the way, if you are in any doubt as to the power these 'employees' have in your change effort.

Employees – who, of course, are everyone, top leadership and change team included – need to own three main objectives with regard to change:

- to develop their individual capacity for change. This means having the intellectual strength, the emotional openness and the attitudinal resilience to accept what is happening. It also means developing the new skills and competence that the Vision implies

- to be involved in the program – to listen, to attend, to be open

- to participate – to offer information and ideas, to join together with others to solve problems as they arise, to challenge the status quo, to put their new learning into practice and above all to offer feedback on how the change is working at all levels of the company; in short, to own the change.

KILLER QUESTIONS

If 'change management' is such a critical skill in business today, why *doesn't* everyone in this organization have 'helping change' mentioned in their job specification?

Great followership

There is no shortage of advice on what great leadership looks like. What would great followership look like?

Here's an idea for a Followership Compact:

- I'll always attempt to see the bigger picture and act in the best interests of that picture.

- I'll balance the short term pain that these changes may inflict on me with the long term benefit that we seek to bring about.

- I will take whatever actions are appropriate to bring the Vision about.

- I'll seek to know what is expected of me and ask for feedback on whether I'm achieving it.

- I will look for ways to develop my understanding and competence, even if this means moving outside of my comfort zone.

- I will offer encouragement when things are working well.

- I'll help my colleagues when they become confused, negative, disaffected.

- I will always tell my leader when he's talking bullshit. Good followership does not mean blind obedience. The status quo needs to be challenged if it is weakening our path to the Vision.

- I'll offer advice from my expertise at the best time for the project.

- I'll give information freely, especially to those who I know can do something about it.

- If responsibility and authority are offered to me, I will take them on.

- If I can't do something, I'll explain why, as soon as I can and honestly.

- I will clarify my doubts with those I know can help me rather than express my doubts to those who can't do anything about them.

- I will see myself as playing the role of explorer in this change: I will be testing a new world. I know this needs both courage and willingness to offer feedback.

- I will remain aware that my actions have a great impact on the total health of the change project and the company as a whole; this is both a privilege I am honored with and a warning to myself.

- I will do the best that I can as often as I can.

CEO signs it first. Distribution list: universal. HR redesigns all performance management systems accordingly.

The circle of foxes; other roles in major change programs

Two further roles are often found in major change projects in large organizations. Both Change Sponsors and Sponsor Champions are there to ensure that the change is happening. Both are based on the old-world assumption that

KILLER QUESTIONS

OK I'm prepared to put my career on the line here, because I'm certainly not going to tolerate the status quo. Who's going to unequivocally and publicly demonstrate their support?

people would rather not change at all and need to be hounded into doing so.

Change Sponsors are traditionally in a position of some political power, strong enough that they can decide which changes will happen in which order, and provide sufficient 'air cover' for the work of the change teams. Sponsors use their muscle to keep the change project on time and on budget. Where this role is not taken by the leadership, a separate sponsor may be needed.

Sponsor Champions are those appointed to keep the sponsor engaged, to act as a coach, perhaps, and help maintain their focus on the importance of the project and the sponsor's role in it. Since sponsors will be spending most of their time carrying out their own work, this extra level of insurance might seem like a good idea, especially if your attitude is that you can't trust anyone to do their work unaided.

You might also sometimes hear about *steering committees*, hideous constructs of department heads who get together to divide up the tasks that will get them most prestige and obstruct the tasks that seem the most dangerous to their continuance. Steering committees slow change down, by steering it hard left or hard right consistently. Steering committees exhibit behavior near the top of the organization that would be condemned as 'employee resistance' were it seen lower down the company.

Perhaps if we don't talk about steering committees anymore, they may just go away.

Smart answers to tough questions

Q: What's the point of using consultants?
A: 'One important aspect of change management that consultants provide: the fresh, objective, impartial outsider's perspective that companies need. Consultants also provide the executive coaching and pushing that organizations often require. Another reason ... is the commitment, the renewed energy or boost, provided. An additional factor to consider is that consultants charge for their services, and an organization not wanting to throw money out of the window will work closely with consultants and perhaps pay more attention to their suggestions than those coming from the ranks of regular management or the work force.'
Carr, Hard, Trahant

Then again, those three are consultants, and so am I.

When it comes to employing consultants, all that matters is:

(1) Do you believe in your heart of hearts that the consultants who are pitching to you can deliver the promises outlined above (i.e. do you trust them as human beings or do you put your trust in their CV and client list)?

(2) Are you sure that the people you employ can deliver the same benefits without outside help?

10

Aligning the Organization: Part 6

SUSTAINING CHANGE THROUGH LEARNING

'Learning is not compulsory; neither is survival ...'

W. Edwards Deming

All change initiatives suffer, variously, from disinterest, cynicism, boredom, apathy, a lack of energy, a dispersal of energy into other areas and concerns. They are launched on a champagne toast of optimism and promise, but sooner or later, when the initial thrill has gone, they run into trouble. In fact, many change initiatives are left to die in this graveyard of human indifference. When people in the organization begin to display uncomfortable behaviors and attitudes – such as disinterest, cynicism, boredom, apathy etc. – it is taken as a very bad sign that things are not working, and so we pull the plug.

In fact most human activities share this pattern of rise and fall – egg-and-spoon races, DIY efforts in the home, sexual intercourse. We always start bigger and faster than we are able to sustain. Change initiatives are no different.

This idea of the natural, cyclical ebb and flow of things also holds for the growth of companies. Many people who are fortunate enough to have been part of the birth of a company look back on those as the halcyon days.

The halcyon creation days are those nearest to the softer areas of business – they are born out of ideals, values, beliefs, ambition, dreams. Once out into the world, they collect a tougher coating. The first invoice may remain framed on the wall as a keepsake memento, but it also brings with it the first cheque, the first bank account, the first customer expectation of continued service, the first bank charges, the first rent payment, the first payroll deadline. Making things happen for the first time gives way to the need to 'keep things going' – keep the money coming in, keep the customers happy, keep meeting the deadline. We stop creating and start sustaining.

I remember the first weeks of my own company start-up as being multi-faceted and rich in experience. They were amazing times. There was a great deal of work to do and ridiculously long hours to pull – but this was matched by a huge amount of spontaneous teamwork and mutual support. There was newness everywhere – first phone, first customer, first invoice, first cheque – which we framed. The thrill was partly that of seeing a dream come into reality; partly that of fearing that it might all collapse. It all seemed so young – boisterous and fragile at the same time. Most of all, though, it was so much fun. Now I look back and I think: where did the fun go?

Designer, new media start-up

Creation energy is easier to harness and move than that of Sustenance energy. Creativity is about new things, which is fun and challenging and positive. Everything is thrilling at the creation stage, there's loads of energy to spare. Sustaining things after you have created them requires a whole raft of other qualities, such as patience, serenity, forgiveness, faith. All of these are beautiful human values, but slower, calmer, than those associated with the heat of birth and creation. They are also less common in business than the fun and passion associated with the creation stage.

Your change initiative will also be subject to the rise and fall of creation and sustenance energy. It is, logically, impossible to keep change new, but it is possible to keep things fresh.

This, and the next chapter, describe two (complementary) ways of doing so.

The learning wheel: keeping change moving

- Change is cyclical

- Learning is cyclical

- Change is learning.

The top–down assumptions of many traditional change methodologies may seem unrealistic if you're not an incoming CEO or a new leader granted extraordinary powers. And not all change in companies is cataclysmic, revolutionary or major. Change is anything that is different from now. Change is what you do when you learn or when you solve a problem. In that sense, change is your job, anybody's job.

How do you ensure any project or team you are part of is learning and open to change continuously?

Answer: The Learning Wheel. It starts, simply enough, with asking a question. Change doesn't occur to suit our change models. It may be difficult to find or create a suitable start point for a vision–analysis–implement model. It may be impossible to follow a linear, ordered sequence of change program activities. But there is never a time when you *can't* ask a question about your work or team. That's why this learning is not necessarily transactional – what new skill or fact do we need to acquire? – but is transformational – what are we producing and what might improve?

And you can ask a learning question in good times or bad. Why do we always need to be facing a crisis to be forced to change?

Change is what you kick into motion when you ask a question

Change can truly be continuous when it takes us on a deepening exploration of our experience. Being interested in what we do – no, more, being fascinated in what we do and what happens to us – is a prerequisite to leading a more productive, purposeful and fun workplace.

The horrible alternative possibility is that you can do a great deal of changing, and not actually learn anything at all.

Understanding learning as the driver of change puts the organization back in control. Rather than being buffeted about by fractious shifts in the external environment which it wishes never happened, the organization it-self, ever curious about itself, ever keen to improve, becomes its own source of renewal.

A leader's job is to ask questions. There is an argument for saying that the only function of leadership is to find out how best to ask the most strategic questions, and how best to create an organization which answers them.

- What are we doing well?
- How can we capture what we do well for when times are tougher?
- What can we do better?
- Why did that happen?
- What can we do next?
- What sort of person should we employ?
- What can we avoid?
- What do we avoid?
- What might we more aware of?
- Where did the fun go?
- Where are we headed?
- Are we stretching ourselves?
- Are we complacent?
- Are we working too hard?
- What are we scared of?
- What are we learning?
- What can we do to make decisions quicker?
- What can we do to improve quality?
- What can we do to meet customer expectations better?
- What are our customers wanting today?
- What are our customers wanting tomorrow?
- Where else might they go for that and why?
- Who are we?
- Who are we pretending to be?
- What can we do to get more passion into work?
- What can we do to get more creativity into work?

- Is what we do deep and complex enough?
- Is it too complicated?
- Is it simple enough?
- Is it too chaotic?
- Is it too ordered?
- Is it too safe?
- Are we on budget?
- Are we on time?
- Where are the costs?
- What are the profits?
- What is our return on investment?
- Where is the value?
- Where is the purpose?
- Where is the love?
- What gets in the way?
- Do we dream enough?
- Do we analyze enough?
- Do we think enough?
- Do we feel enough?
- What can we do to break down barriers?
- Do we ever discuss the 'undiscussables'?
- What are we doing about the past?
- What are we doing about the future?
- How are we spending our time?
- How are we spending our money?
- How do we treat each other?
- What do we take for granted?
- What are we preserving?
- Is it clear what we believe in?
- Is it working?
- Is it right?
- Is it true?
- Are we underselling ourselves?
- What opportunities are we missing?
- What impact am I having?

- How can I verify that I'm understood?
- Do I inspire?
- Do I delegate enough?
- Do I believe it?
- How can we encourage ownership?
- How do I show trust?
- What do I hold on to too tightly?
- Who could give us a new perspective?

Four stages to learning

So, the Learning Wheel has four stages, the first being the **Question**.

Charles Handy, who drew this same simple learning model in his book *Inside Organizations*, reminds us of the old adage that those who ask no questions get told no lies – maybe – but they also do not add to their understanding of the world. Questions set the wheel turning.

Then comes **Theory** – the question demands an answer. Hypotheses are created to suggest a way forward.

Theories leap off the page into reality, and at no other time, when we take **Action**. Actions solidify our ideas and dreams, shows us how the Theory works out in front of us rather than in the front of our mind's eye.

Our Actions stumble around our lives, stupid, unchecked and possibly harmful unless we Reflect on their appropriateness or effectiveness.

Reflection allows us to find out whether the Action needs to be adjusted or the Theory needs to be tweaked. Or perhaps it would be better if we asked a new Question?

Question, Theory, Action, Reflection: it's the rhythm of learning

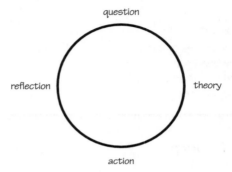

The challenge you face as a manager or leader is to keep the learning cycle moving effectively. To do that, you need to cultivate certain conditions or habits at each stage.

To generate Questions, you need to inculcate a habit of Curiosity

Curiosity killed the cat only in a tale made up by a mother exasperated by the innate inquisitiveness of her toddler. (Actually stupidity kills cats, or kidney failure.) Curiosity is that driving need to know which catapults us out of dependent child consciousness and into self-aware, learning maturity. Curiosity creates smart human beings. It is said that half of everything a person knows has been learnt by age 7. What tends to take over then is the Ego's assurances that any more knowledge would threaten the hard-won psychological status quo or is just not worth the bother of acquiring. Add to this the immersion of most of us in schools which favor facts and tests over experimentation and exploration, and you'll understand why little curiosity remains into adulthood.

Curiosity has to be stimulated in order to drive any learning at all. Curiosity expresses itself as questioning

- why did we do *that* again?

- what have been the causes of this?

but it gains its piercing intensity from the scope and quantity of the questions. Learning organizations require constant questions, the outward expression of never being satisfied with the way things have gone or are going. Learning organizations also require deep and wide questions, questions which get under the surface of the current problems to the habits, patterns and weaknesses that underlie them. Safe questions maintain safety. Asking the probing, simple questions such as 'why?' and 'why not?' shows the urge towards safety to be hugely limiting and possibly dangerous to the organization. The old business world was about optimizing production – doing the same thing over and over again but cheaper than your competitors. The new world is about maximizing imagination – asking the questions that your competitors have missed and exploiting the answers creatively and fast.

To generate Theories, you need to inculcate a habit of Creativity

Questions demand answers. The mind is usually very good at responding to that need, either by providing a top of the head solution, or at the very least, the polite truth 'I don't know'. (Actually, 'I don't know' is not something you hear said much in organizations – the Ego feels vulnerable when it confesses ignorance). The trouble is that knee-jerk responses, although they fill the silence, may not get us very far in times of trouble. The danger with Answers is that they might well kill Questions stone dead, in the same way that decisions murder alternatives.

We need *lots* of possible answers, not the same ones that have brought us to this pass in the first place. Nurturing a habit of Creativity pushes your people to look beyond the shallow, easy answer and to come up with new ideas, open new doors, create new opportunities.

Creative ideas enrol others – they excite and engage their audience. They set up stretch goals by creating new possibilities that were not there before. And creativity, from its nature as a solution-provider, gives assurance that change is possible and achievable.

Increasing people's capacity for creativity allows them to get around the instinct to let someone else solve a problem.

To produce Action, you need to inculcate a habit of Courage

All the creativity in the world will do you no good without the courage to implement your ideas. Courage gives people the will to push past obstacles, to take risks, to stretch themselves. Courage is the innate ability that we all possess to operate beyond the Ego, and its demands to keep us safe, secure, liked, respectable. Courage is not something you learn, it is something you access, since you already have it inside (this is what you learn on an outdoor training event). At the same time, courage is strengthened by repeated excursions outside the comfort zone, and weakened by a refusal to go there.

Courage is what you will need to present solutions which are contrary to organizational culture or personal conditioning. Courage is what you will need to put your reputation on the line for the sake of the change. Courage is what you will need to tackle bureaucratic resistance or political humbug. An environment which understands and encourages courageous actions without recrimination allows others to follow you. That momentum helps to ensure that you don't end up a dead hero.

See this book's information on Fear for ideas on how to release your own courage, but remember the biggest fear most companies generate is that you will lose your job unless you play the game. Act like you are a person of independent means and massive personal wealth who was just working for the fun of it (which, after Chapter One, you know you are anyway) and you'd be surprised by how much you'll achieve.

To encourage Reflection, you need to inculcate a habit of Candor and Honesty

The dispiriting sight of the politician avoiding a straight answer to a straight question is almost enough to push every one of us into a lifetime of honesty, but evidently not quite enough. There's plenty of places to hide in an organization, and the Truth often gets hidden out of sight and out of mind. We find miraculous ways of either not telling or not hearing the Truth. This capacity for avoidance at work is matched only by our shameless ability to share it in the pub or the coffee house.

Change is complex enough in organizations without suppressing our ability to say which Actions really worked and which didn't, which Theories are doomed from the start and which embody some hope, and which Questions keep us in the dark and which show us the way to the light. Without Candor, the Learning Cycle is turned into a Spinning Top, fast-moving, undoubtedly colorful, strangely engaging yet ultimately pointless.

Reflection seals in learning. Reflection which cheats on or mangles the Truth seals in waste and frustration.

Curiosity, Creativity, Courage, Candor: this is the outer ring, the locomotive force, of the learning cycle.

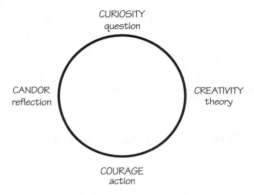

CURIOSITY
question

CREATIVITY
theory

COURAGE
action

CANDOR
reflection

'St Luke's changes each year, because its owners change ...These owners come in to St Luke's on the understanding that we keep exploring. If we ever stop exploring, we will be as guilty as everyone else of finding a formula and sticking to it. Formulas work in the short term, like prescriptions. But if you stick to them, you become increasingly immune to the effects of the changing outside world. You allow your company to age slowly in comparison to the changes outside ... You know you company is ageing when the proportion of people who want to inflict change is smaller than those who want to rely on the practices of the good old days ...Our Vision – 'To Open Minds' – is there before us to remind us what will happen when we stop exploring.'

Open Minds: 21 Business Lessons and Innovations from St Luke's, Andy Law

Charles Handy is a person who asks the Big Questions.

This calmly communicative and warm-hearted 'social philosopher' (he long ago began to successfully blur the distinction between business concerns and those of wider human existence) began his expansive career at Shell and there learned much about the assumptions and beliefs which drive large organizations. Even in the past, he must have sensed that being big was not the way forward. He spent some time learning at MIT in the era of Ed Schein and other human relations experts, and took up a post at the London Business School where he taught from 1972. Handy has also been the Warden of St George's House in Windsor Castle and a chairman of the Royal Society for the Encouragement of Arts, Manufactures and Commerce.

Handy's breakthrough book was *The Age of Unreason* in which he suggested for the first time and most strongly, that the only way we were going to meet the challenges of unpredictable, wrenching, discontinuous change was by learning to change ourselves. A new type of thinking and behavior was especially needed and a new challenge set for the smart careerist:

'... discontinuous change requires discontinuous, upside-down thinking to deal with it, even if both thinkers and thoughts appear absurd at first sight.'

Handy is not just content to label the paradoxes of our complex world; he provokes us to search for personal and organizational fulfillment and knows it can be achieved 'if we can understand what is happening and are prepared to be different'.

Handy's particular talent is for expressing possible solutions for the need to do things differently in images that have seared their way into the business literature's memory bank. Handy's is a world of shamrock organizations, inverted doughnuts, portfolio careers, Chinese contracts, sigmoid curves and empty raincoats. The latter haunting image, inspired by a sculpture by Judith Shea, expresses for Handy the fear that 'if economic progress means that we become anonymous cogs in the machine, then progress is an empty promise.'

SMART PEOPLE
TO HAVE ON
YOUR SIDE:

CHARLES
HANDY

Handy's writing is superbly readable, but 'underneath its benign and positive style', as *The Director* magazine put it, 'lies radical intent.' His most thought-provoking work, in my opinion, is *The Hungry Spirit*, pushing us as it does towards a contemplation of 'the meaning of business', without which all this change we're going through might appear an absurd and pointless nightmare:

What good can it possibly do to pile up riches which you cannot conceivably use, and what is the point of the efficiency needed to create those riches if one third of the world's workers are now unemployed or under-employed, as the ILO calculates? And where will it end, this passion for growth? If we go on growing at our present rate we will be buying sixteen times as much of everything in 100 years' time. Even if the world's environment can tolerate the burden, what are we going to do with all that stuff? Seventy corporations now rank bigger than many a nation state. Does that matter? ... The apparent lack of concern about these problems from those in powerful places smacks of complacency ... I am concerned by the absence of a more transcendent view of life and the purposes of life, and by the prevalence of the economic myth which colors all that we do. Money is the means of life and not the point of it. There must be something that we can do to restore the balance.

The son of a rector, Handy does not just preach. An advocate of challenging us all to know when enough is enough, he sits down with his wife at the beginning of the year and estimates what income they will need to do the things that they would like to do that year. When he has earned that figure, he flatly refuses to take on any more work, even though the temptation to give another lucrative speech to an audience of CEOs must be considerable.

Handy has a secondary career as a contributor to BBC Radio Four's 'Thought for the Day' on the breakfast news programme *Today*. His gentle chiding has probably induced many a sleepy-eyed listener to think big thoughts – and ask big questions of themselves – as they make another dull trip to the office.

The inner circle is naturally linked. Theories that are not the children of Questions are just gimmicks. Actions that are not the results of Theories are random experimentation. Reflections which do not test actions are mere philosophy, which is fine in its setting but inappropriate in the pragmatic reality of work.

So too is the outer circle linked and cumulative. Your Questions, for example, driven by Curiosity, need to be both Creative and Courageous if they are to demonstrate that you mean business. They need to be creative enough to show that you are thinking in new ways about old problems and courageous enough to show that you are prepared to move beyond the cozy surface of what ails the company.

All aspects of the wheel are fueled by Candor.

(... well, one can dream.)

Kick-starting the Learning Wheel in your company

'Always the beautiful answer who asks a more beautiful question.'

e e cummings

Remember that the quality of the questions you ask determines the quality of the answers – and ultimately, through Action, the outcome. Compare the probable learning cycles generated by the two questions: 'they always are so cynical; what's the use?' and 'they are always so cynical; how can I learn more about their fears and doubts or motivators so that I can make a better attempt next time?' Or how about the difference between 'there's so much change about: what will I do if I lose my job?' and 'what can I learn here now which will increase my value whether I keep my job here or move somewhere else?' Ask constructive questions.

- Your outcomes are shaped by the questions you ask – but they are also affected by those you fail to ask. Challenge your people at every meeting: 'what might we be missing here?'

- Prod curiosity into being. Ask at least one person every day 'How about ...'; 'Have you considered ...'

- Even better, ask 'What questions are *you* asking today?'

- You can kill curiosity by threatening or appearing to threaten. How much is yours a culture of 'be right first time'. How OK is it to display ignorance or say 'I don't know'?

- How relaxed and playful is your culture? How patient and forgiving? Are mistakes learnt from and laughed at (in time) – or are they held over people like an axe? If people cannot be themselves, if they are constantly fighting to maintain an Ego mask of invincibility or expertise, then you will not get curiosity. Think of your own curious childhood, nagging your parents with 'why, why, why?'. If at any time your parents turned round and said: 'you stupid child, how come you don't know that already?' or 'you asked exactly the same thing last week, don't you ever learn anything?' or 'stop bothering me, I have something far more important to do' or 'I'm beginning to think your sister's right. You *are* beyond hope – I'm going to take you back to where we got you and ask for a replacement' then they would have killed stone dead your curiosity. (By the way, if your childhood was like that, I'm sorry to have used you as a case study. I'll get your permission for the next edition.)

- How positive is your culture? How easy is it to know what's working well rather than what's failing or struggling? People often focus on the negative or bad news – think of the nature of the rumor network – and it's amazing how companies simply play into that fact by majoring there. How much good news does your company notice board or bulletin board have? How much info is there on contracts won, customers retained, brave decisions taken, corporate principles or values defended, extraordinary service acknowledged? And another very simple test of how positive your culture: how often do your meetings begin with the question: 'Tell me – what's going well around here?'

- Are the stars in your company resting on past achievements and knowledge or always looking for new learning?

- Consider how much your systems and processes reflect all this. How much opportunity do your recruitment interviews, for example, give for candidates to display their curiosity? How much genuine, unforced curiosity, do you show towards them?

- Ask people what they want. Give them that to the best of your ability. Keep asking them what they want. This is the first principle of motivation (and staff retention).

- Ask people what they need to learn in order to play their part better in moving the company towards its Vision. Provide it. This is the first principle of staff development.

- How open are *you* to questioning? If some asks you to explain yourself, are you defensive, dismissive, judgmental?

- Give people formal time to share expertise, experience and learning.

- Maximize diversity. Mix genders, races, persuasions, viewpoints. Prepare to take people to a level of understanding above any immediate conflict that may arise. And make sure you do have diversity and not homogeneity, which is a curiosity killer. I went to an international conference once. The organizers kept telling us how proud they were of bringing together such a diverse group of people. I looked around. We were all pretty much middle class, 35–50, chiefly white. What they meant was that some of us had travelled a long way to be there, but that isn't diversity. We learnt little at that conference because we were preaching to each other, and we were already converted.

- Make time for job swaps or sharing or rotation. Everybody gets a day on the help desk. Everybody gets a day shadowing the boss.

- Demonstrate that everything in your company is transitory (which it is) and up for change. Since nothing lasts for ever, encourage people to challenge even the most established practices. Ask 'Can we do it better?' about everything, regularly.

- Present information in interesting ways and with context and relevance. Every piece of data should have a clear implication, and a clear set of considerations that need to be given to it. 'Here's our stock flow forecast. This means X, Y and Z. What we need to do because of it is A, B and C. Any suggestions?'

- People deaden their own curiosity through low self-esteem – so be generous (and specific) (and honest) (and public) in your praise.

- People deaden their own curiosity through a belief that someone else is actually going to do the work or get the kudos. Learn to delegate well –

both authority and responsibility – so that people have to stretch themselves to achieve the goal. Make it clear that your delegation sets the 'what' and the 'by when' and 'with what priority' and 'to what standard' (and always checks: 'is that all clear and understood?') but not the 'how'. If they ask you 'how?' – say 'I dunno – go and find out.'

- People deaden their curiosity when they can't understand. Train everyone in attentive listening skills and learning how to learn.

- People deaden their curiosity when they can't present their ideas well. Train everyone in first class communication and presentation skills.

- People deaden their curiosity when they lose a sense of wonder about what is happening around them. Make work an adventure. Set huge goals. Encourage big dreams. Take risks. Have fun. In other words, allow people to realize their potential, instead of restricting human potential to the most persistent fears and ingrained habits.

'Never lose a holy curiosity.'

Albert Einstein

'Learning occurs between a fear and a need. On the one hand, we feel the need to change if we are to accomplish our goals. On the other hand, we feel the anxiety of facing the unknown and unfamiliar. To learn significant things, we must suspend some basic notions about our worlds and ourselves. That is one of the most frightening propositions for the Ego.'

Peter Senge

Smart quotes

Peter M. Senge is Director of the Center for Organizational Learning at MIT's Sloan School of Management and a founding partner of the management consulting and training firm Innovation Associates. In 1990 he released *The Fifth Discipline: The Art and Practice of the Learning Organization* (Doubleday/Currency) and instigated an enormous amount of discussion and theorizing about an entity which has almost steadfastly refused to appear. Learning organizations are a bit like the Loch Ness Monsters. Everyone wants to be a believer in them, but very, very few have ever seen one.

Senge himself has an answer to this. 'There is no such thing as a learning organization', he explains, which seems a pretty brave thing for a guru to say about the thing that is most associated with his name, and which earns most of his fees. By this he means that 'a learning organization' is as much a vision as an external reality – and that what matters is the quality of questions and experimentation that the term provokes in us. Inspired by the search to become 'a learning organization', many companies (Ford, AT&T, Federal Express amongst them) are making brave experiments in terms of communication, co-creating of vision, democratization, structural redesign and team-working, and in particular being patient enough to seek the systemic origins of the problems they face, rather than hurrying to 'fix' the problem symptoms as soon as they arise.

Companies are certainly moving a lot faster in these directions than had Senge never coined the term.

Four departments that never were

Department Q

Purpose:

- to listen to the world to hear what it is asking for/demanding of the company and translate that into learning or goal-oriented strategic intents

- to plot and, as far as possible, predict changes in the environment, thus focusing the organization in the 'right' direction

- to disseminate the reality that asking one question often leads to seven others; and that, therefore, frustration and confusion are an unavoidable side effect of living in paradoxical, constantly changing times and *not* the result of us being stupid.

Department T

Purpose:

- to promulgate both/and (rather than either/or) thinking

- to integrate and synthesize knowledge from many diverse sources to provide a knowledge bank of possible solutions

- to respond to the intelligence provided by Dept Q and produce new, innovative processes, new, innovative products and better old ones.

Department A

Purpose:

- to keep a constant check on the beliefs, assumptions and practices of the organization and prevent stagnation, complacency and other blockages developing

- to provide a database of skills and tools and a pool of specialist resource, both internal and external, to implement change

- to ensure that the new concepts are being used to peruse new objectives, and set goals and measures for the same.

Department R

Purpose:

- to provide understanding of and for the whole, through tracking patterns of meaning and purpose in the company's experience

- to provide a leadership of balance, judgment and reflectiveness

- to influence an environment of support and safety, such that the big, *dangerous* questions can be asked.

11

Aligning the Organization: Part 7

MAKING CHANGE FUN

'A spirit of play, a spirit of rebelliousness, a sense of adventure, an eagerness to challenge and be challenged, these are the things that expose our brains to those experiences that make us grow new neural connections. But when a leader is already running a successful business, it takes a special kind of courage to remain childlike.'

Rewiring the Corporate Brain, Danah Zohar

Being deadly serious about fun

This chapter, tucked away near the back of this book, lest the fun get in the way of the real work, posits two deadly serious challenges.

- Firstly a challenge to You as Smart Manager/Leader/Team Member:

  How can you create an environment in your organization such that your colleagues want to come to work in the morning?

- Secondly, there's a challenge to the personal You:

  How can you reinvent the disproportionately high percentage of your life which you spend working to create real purpose and meaning and satisfaction, rather than work remaining a bulky and necessary hindrance to 'real life'?

I would guess that we'll only ever be in a position to take on the first challenge when we have faced up to the second.

Reinventing work

Over the years, I have seen two common and recurring strategies for making work fun. The first uses the fun as a sort of bandage, covering the work under layers of humor and entertainment. Pranks are common during working hours, everyone must have a Dilbert cartoon pinned up in their cubicle, and heavy drinking between 6 p.m. and the 8.30 p.m. back to Surburbi-town is almost compulsory. This strategy essentially sees work as toil, a burden which, though it cannot be shaken off and must be endured, can at least be made tolerable with a joke and a merry song. This is a strategy which the British are well groomed for. It is the war spirit. Chin up. Don't let the bastards grind you down.

The second strategy is quite different and is the Smart Strategy. It sees work in a quite different light. It accepts work as a part of life, rather than an interruption to it, and therefore embraces it with all its difficulty and pressure and frustrations. This strategy has three guiding principles:

- that the purpose of work is to discover and express who we are, both as individuals and as social beings. Work allows us to grow and develop our talents, to learn from how we strive to give birth to our ideas and to combine with others to produce something greater than what alone we could achieve

- that we learn as much from life's (and therefore work's) problems and dark times as ever we do from its flashes of joy and brilliance

- that expecting work to be fun all the time is a fantasy with no chance of ever becoming reality.

In other words, for the people who follow this second strategy, the fun is *in* the work, not separate from it. Making work fun for them is based on an internal, attitudinal shift as much any change in the external environment.

Elements of fun

Listening to people who tell me that their work is fun has taught me other things too.

What do they mean by fun? And how do they find it?

The first thing to note about this fun thing that it is an entirely subjective phenomenon. What is fun for me is not necessarily fun for you. Stamp collecting is fun for you. Me, I get my kicks from black-run snow boarding. That fun is subjective and personal is a truth we should accept as readily as saying that what I find funny you may not, but it has enormous implications for those of you who are trying to create a corporate culture which accepts and encourages work to be fun. How are you going to find a 'fun' which is acceptable to all? Are you really going to be able to tolerate all the diversity of subjective fun that a team, a department or a whole company might contain?

So that's the first element of fun – its inherent subjectivity. Perhaps this explains why it's always fun to find out what other people find fun. Just ask.

The second thing I learnt about fun at work is that, whatever it is, it usually fits into one of the following four categories:

1. *Connection*

   Whatever it is, it's fun because of the relationships built with other people, or perhaps because of a connection to some cause or purpose.

2. *Achievement*

   Whatever it is, it's fun because something positive is achieved as a result of doing it – e.g. a creative solution, an experience of personal growth, a success, a result, a win.

3. *Joy*

   Whatever it is, it's fun because it sparks a feeling of energy, 'buzz', well-being or excitement, for example through the use of humor, games playing and entertainment.

4. *Freedom*

> Whatever it is, it's fun because the participants are free of (or break through) either real or imagined personal, social or cultural constraints

A short answer, then, to the question 'how do we make work fun?' would be to say we should work on maximizing experiences which fit in one or more of the four categories above. That's a short and simple answer, but not an easy one. Organizations provide constant opportunities to 'connect', for example, but 'connection' describes the *quality* of people's interactions with others (e.g. in terms of empathy, honesty, conflict resolution) as much as the *quantity*.

Three core beliefs that hinder fun

I have also found that there are certain fundamental assumptions about work and organizations that get in the way of our attempts to make work fun. Here are three.

1. The Organizational Cult of Deferment

states that:

It's fine to have fun, of course it is, it's just that we're too busy now. So, if you wouldn't mind, please have your fun after 5.30 p.m. Or at the weekend. Or on holiday. Or in retirement, just before you drop down dead after slaving your life away here. Thank you for your attention.

The deferment of pleasure is what recovering addicts are conditioned into when they are trying to break their heroin or crack habit. In their case, it's perhaps an understandable approach to their condition, but it strikes me as psychologically limited in a healthy individual.

But perhaps our organizations haven't always wanted healthy individuals, which brings us to ...

2. *The* Neotonization *of People*

which is a big, fancy word meaning the genetic and developmental retardation of development and is a term from biology. Dogs are neotonized wolves – they are retarded wild animals, stuck and now forcibly bred into a permanent domesticity. Cats, I suppose, are neotonized wildcats – they share primitive instincts for a more fully developed hunter/forager existence, but in reality all they do is sleep on your lap and lick their backsides ...

Generations of hierarchical structure, command and control cultures and the ridiculous solemnization of business by the few who have the most power has neotonized too many people. Organizations don't have wolves or wildcats (independent, self-reliant, powerful). They have the tamer versions of the same thing (dependent, selfish, weak) ... Wolves may be scarier to manage, but they're better equipped to survive and thrive. And wolves wouldn't tolerate Core Belief 1 above.

3. *The Measurement of Everything*

which maybe is always going to be true in a world where everything is focused on the bottom line (which will be sad), but that doesn't mean to say that we are already in possession of all the measuring tools we'll ever need. A Fun-ometer may be difficult to design, but I'll bet you if Bill Gates turned his mind to it, we'd snap it up no problem.

Why bother with fun at work after all?

Because it may be becoming a competitive necessity in a changing world of work, which has moved from the age of production into the era of innovation and information. Along with that transition has come a shift in emphasis from organizational control to individual potential.

In the old world of production and command, the old certainties were what distinguished a company in the eyes of its prospective employees – salary, promotion, perks, with size the most important factor in all three categories.

Finding and retaining the best people now, however, means that organizations have to become comfortable with the shifting, subjective world of environment, values and personal needs, since these are the things that have increasing meaning for us all.

Perhaps we'll need a new definition of 'corporate culture':

from

the way we do things around here – so get used to it, keep your nose clean and all will be well

to

whatever turns you on whilst you're here and whilst we're trying to get the best out of you.

It always seems to be like that for the Creative Directors in ad agencies anyway. Maybe their relationship with their employers – where space to innovate, explore and play is expected and granted – provides a glimpse of the 'looser' corporate environment which fun at work demands.

Eight things you can do to bring a looser, more relaxed and fun-friendly environment

1.   Poke fun at yourself, yourselves, your company.

Organizations can be stupefyingly dull and stupid places. For a change, don't get angry. Laugh. Satirize. Caricature. Mimic.

SMART PEOPLE
TO HAVE ON
YOUR SIDE:

ROSABETH
MOSS KANTOR

Rosabeth Moss Kantor is one of very few females who can challenge the likes of Peters, Pascale and Handy in terms of international influence and renown. Holder of the 1960 Chair as Professor of Business Administration at the Harvard Business School, she was also editor of the Harvard Business Review from 1989 to 1992. Under her stewardship, the HBR was a finalist in the National Magazine for General Excellence in 1991.

Like Handy, Kantor's writings are humane and grounded in sociology, opening up the potential for truly people-based organizations. Hers is the notion of the post-entrepreneurial firm which manages to combine the traditional strengths of a large organization with the flexible speed of a smaller organization. At the centre of this is a positive reading of change. Look up 'change' in the index of her first really popular work *The Change Masters* and you will find yourself directed to another entry. *'Change, see Innovation'*, it says.

Kantor regrets the 'quiet suffocation of the entrepreneurial spirit in segmentalist companies' and encourages empowerment: 'the degree to which the opportunity to use power effectively is granted to or withheld from individuals is one operative difference between those companies which stagnate and those that innovate.'

Lately, she has offered a four-part prescription for those companies which are intent on mastering change ('the most important thing a leader can help their organization do'). These companies, she says, must be:

- *focused*: to pick only those areas in which you can be excellent in all dimensions
- *fast*: to increase your innovation of goods to market speed, your processing of information and decisions speed and the recovery speed at which you respond and fix problems
- *flexible*: to employ the broadest of job categories, minimize bureaucracy and exploit cross-boundary team working
- *friendly*: not just the friendliness that aids collaboration within the organization, but the friendliness which build trusting links with their customers and suppliers.

She also adds a fifth F suggesting that unless corporations can maximize the pleasure and satisfaction that work can bring an individual, then they are not going to find anybody to do that work, because the pressures of change can be overwhelming. Her fifth F stands for *fun*, but I can't think that this is an idea that will ever catch on, do you?

2. Celebrate often, for the bizarrest of reasons. Celebrate 'as if' you've finished because you know that the Organizational Cult of Deferment will otherwise make you put it off. Celebrate events in people's private lives as well as milestones in the change project.

3. Banish dress-down Friday. Have a 'progressively fewer clothes during the week' week. Or at least pretend to.

4. Practice random acts of kindness.

5. Hold regular brainstorms (which themselves can be fun if you do them right – and if you don't, invest in someone who can teach you how) on different themes: 'how to make meetings more fun'; 'how to reward our staff at a cost of less than £50 per time' etc.

6. Learn something fun together. Juggling. Skiing. Shiatsu massage.

7. As a team, give something to the community. Offer mentorship to a school, training sessions at a job club. Clean a stream.

8. Hold competitions which are aimed at providing you with another 8, 18, 81, 888 ways to loosen up. Competition One: the most creative ways to connect with colleagues/our customers/our purpose. Competition Two: the most creative ways to celebrate achievement/achieve on this project. Competition Three: the most creative ways to free people at work. Competition Four: the most creative ways to bring joy into our organization.

Change is worth celebrating

For Smart people, connection is the first element of fun at work.

Connection can mean a chance meeting that brought about a stimulating discussion and the seed of a brilliant idea (which is why BA's new HQ is designed around a walkway called The Street, deliberately encouraging people to experience chance encounters).

Connection could mean that sense of purpose you feel when you remember, if only for the moment, that your work really does add value to the world. It could also describe a great team meeting in the middle of an otherwise nondescript day; or the charity mini-marathon four of you did last year.

I'd like to spend the rest of this chapter considering a more formal sort of connection – the corporate celebration.

Celebrations and the ceremonies they encapsulate provide an opportunity to mark special beliefs, occasions, occurrences or people. They underscore change. They are ancient, universal, multi-cultural phenomena – every human being on the planet has experienced the rhythm and meaning of ceremony. But they remain under-utilized in the business world. This part of the chapter suggests that they could become a crucial element in any change programme.

Change brings loss; an appropriate celebration could be critical in allowing people to mark transition and let go of the past (that's what we do at funerals and wakes). Change brings creativity; a ceremony or party is an

---

FUNCTIONS OF A CEREMONY

- to bond
- to connect individual to whole, and individual to purpose
- to convey shared values
- to create cultural hero/heroines
- to create share and collect new cultural stories
- to design new cultural rituals or artefacts
- to release tension
- to foster creativity
- to provide closure and ending
- to welcome new people or practices.

---

excellent way of publicly celebrating achievement, marking particular values or behaviors, or simply for welcoming something new into the organizational world (that's what we do at a wedding or baby-naming ceremony). Change happens over time; a celebration could mark significant signposts, stages or cycles (that thick hangover on Jan 1 is a result of doing the same) and at the same time review progress and set new targets.

Each if these needs could be met with some other business practice, of course: a memo here, an email there, a little speech at the end of a meeting. But holding a ceremony or celebration offers you the chance of taking your people out of the rush and push, away from the stress, out of the drudgery and the humdrum. It allows you to spend that precious corporate resource – time – and do something special with it.

In business, celebrations, if they come at all, tend to come at the end of projects or at the end of the year in the dreaded and dreadful office party. These celebrations are often:

- given little or any thought above the purely logistical (who will pick up how much booze from which liquor store when) and barely any to the event's purpose, tone or structure

- held in whatever venue 'will do, given the number of people we have coming'

- characterized by poor-quality materials (vile wine and cheap decorations) which perhaps demonstrate the true attitude of the organization toward the event

- marked by 'a few words', hurriedly prepared and badly delivered, from a senior person who probably has little connection to the people gathered (and shows this in his actions)

- hurried into, hurried out of, passed over quickly.

The intention can't be faulted. Instinctively we know that getting people together at the same time in the same place is good for group spirit. We know that such a gathering can be enhanced by food, drink or artefacts. And even the most feeble standard business celebration contains ritual – the award ceremony, the speech-making. In this way, even the most embarrassing office party shares the same components as the most exalted and focused ceremony. So why don't we push ourselves to learn how much better we could make them?

It is time to realize that hosting good gatherings is a skill and may even be an art form. Most businesses don't or can't do it well. Companies think a gathering has gone well if most of the invited or expected people simply turn up. Even worse, they think that they are being generous just by holding 'parties' at all, howsoever awful they turn out to be.

Ritual and ceremony are the universal forms of celebration.

Almost all meaningful ceremonies have the same characteristics. Think of a ceremony you're all familiar with: the Opening of the Olympic Games.

Its main attributes are:

- *care* enough to demonstrate the importance of the occasion – everybody knows what the ceremony is intended to achieve and how it will do it. It has been given budget and resources. It has been planned, long in advance. Every element has been rehearsed – not just the most visible elements like the dancing troupe, but every minor detail which helps the event run smoothly, from ticket collection, crowd control and dispersal, to toilet-cleaning

- an appropriate *venue* – in the Games' case, of course, it is the Olympic Stadium. Perhaps there aren't too many choices of where to put 70,000 people, but note that a Stadium is appropriate anyway. It is monumental – its sheer scale matches the sense of occasion. It focuses a diverse audience on specific locations and also – by virtue of the encircling red running track and field markings – sets people thinking of the ultimate reason they are there: the sporting activities to come

- the use of powerful *music* – to set the tone, focus the audience, mark stages of the ceremony

- the use of deliberate *silence*, for similar reasons

- *ritualized or stylized behavior* – in the form of processions, marching, dance

- *costumes* – the national dress of each country, blazered officials

- *symbology* – the country flags, the five interlocking circles on the Olympic flag, the universal fire, the lone runner

- *storytelling* – it stresses its sense of continuance from the past into the future, its historical and mythical origins, its links to all the peoples of the Earth

- *structure* – the ceremony follows a particular order, just as a church service does

- *aesthetics* – lighting, sounds, colors and shapes produce a beautiful event

- *participation* – the audience members in this and all ceremonies come to observe the ceremony, and to mark the occasion with their presence. When you go to the Olympic Opening Ceremony, you are obviously aware that you are here in a particular place on a particular day – but you are also very aware that thousands did exactly this four years ago, and every year four years over a hundred years. But above all, the ceremony allows one to participate, to join in, whether it be by singing, applauding, cheering, even by holding up that painted card at the right time. It is a collective experience, your one becoming part of the whole

We were laying off a lot of people who had worked together for many years, and we wanted to do something to mark that. Moreover, the department itself was closing down – or rather being changed and merged with others in a new corporate structure. That department had been there since the company was born in the last century. It seemed so feeble to just hold a party. But whenever we contemplated something more 'meaningful', all our little embarrassments came up and we said to ourselves: we're very busy and there's precious little time for ceremonies and rituals in the business world, so we won't do anything ... Eventually we threw the problem open to the whole department. One of the first ideas we got back was the one we did, because it seemed so right. We made a huge coffin out of cardboard and papier mâché, painted it, decorated it, filled it with all sorts of mementoes of the department's history. And on the day in question, we marched it through the department and out into the car park, where we said a speech or two and then burnt it. We played music, sad and happy, like at the beginning of that James Bond film in New Orleans. It wasn't at all macabre. On the contrary, it was very moving and at the same time great, great fun. Then we had the party, and people talked long into the night. When I look back on it, it wasn't just the ceremony that helped people cope with the change. It was joining together to make the coffin. It was like the last piece of team work and the big goodbye.

Project Manager, engineering and environmental consultancy

- *celebration* of themes at once particular and universal – not just skilled athletics for example, but transcendent human values such as striving for excellence, winning, preparation, investment in self, overcoming of odds etc.

Combine all this together and you can appreciate how celebrations appeal to all facets of the human experience – physical, intellectual, emotional and spiritual.

If business celebrations followed just some of theses twelve attributes, they could be used to reconnect people with values and beliefs, create important memories and allow individuals to feel that they are undeniably part of something bigger than their own little job.

Why on earth wouldn't you use them more and more effectively during your change programme?

Change Agent as ceremonialist and great host

A checklist for your next change event:

- What's the purpose of this event:

  - to mark a stage reached?

  - to recognize an achievement or person?

  - to celebrate triumph?

  - to mark ending or loss?

- to reaffirm continuity and succession?

- to play?

- What's the best timing for this event?

- What do we want the audience to do as a result of this event?

- What emotions are we trying to heighten?

- Which emotions are we trying to release?

- What understanding are we trying to convey?

- What's a meaningful concept or theme that aligns with our purpose?

- How can this concept be reflected in:

  - venue?

  - structure/order of event?

  - choice of ritual?

  - choice of speakers/speech?

  - music?

  - room decor?

  - invitation and marketing material?

- dress code?

- prizes/gifts/accessories?

- takeaways/mementoes?

- specialist entertainment/guest ceremonialists – magicians, jugglers, dancers, singers, shamanic medicine women?

- Is our design appealing to all four human aspects? What opportunities will there be for:

  - physical movement?

  - emotional release?

  - new intellectual understanding?

  - spiritual experience?

- How many rehearsals shall we have and when (a number above two is good)?

- How will we plan to deal with the five big resistances before they crop up:

  - Won't we look silly if we do anything more purposeful than stand around having a drink?

  - I don't see the point of getting people together like this (even though I have a Harvard MBA and am bright enough to run a company, there are some times when I'm a bit slow, see).

- It's too much effort.

- We don't have the time.

- I agree with the intention but I'm far too busy for a rehearsal – can't I wing it on the night?

Saying farewell to the past

Smart change masters find it easy to be upbeat and constructive, but they also are sensitive to endings. They know that an event may well have to mark the end of the old way of doing things before they can celebrate the new one.

Here are some ideas on how to make an ending, which is respectful yet clear:

• give it appropriate time and space; messy goodbyes leave things unsaid that fester

Smart quotes

'The starting point for transition is not the outcome but the ending that you will have to make to leave the old situation behind ... The second step is understanding what comes after letting go: the neutral zone. This is the no man's land between the old identity and the new. It's the time when the old way is gone but the new one doesn't feel comfortable yet ... People make a new beginning only if they have made an ending and spent some time in the neutral zone. Yet most organizations try to start with the beginning rather than finishing it.'

Managing Transitions: Making the Most of Change, William Bridges

- make it clear that this is the *ending*

- don't denigrate the past: it is someone's friend

- honor what has gone as a healthy precursor to the present development

- mark the ending with a ceremony: perhaps burn or bury a piece of the past

- give people a piece of the past to take with them as a memento of a good time: don't give the impression it can be brought with us in any other way than this symbolic one

- brush up on Kubler-Ross and make a judgment how far people are along the path to Acceptance.

Acknowledgment

Much of the section on celebration is inspired by Terence Deal & M.K. Key's excellent guide to holding business ceremonies, *Corporate Celebration: Play, Purpose & Profit at Work:* to whom much praise and thanks.

An Almost-Epilogue

Out There: beyond the management of change

So what does the future hold for change? How will we change the way we change?

As always, the question can be answered on two levels: the organization and the individual.

Organizational change will increasingly move from the cycle of goal-oriented improvement (see Chapter 3) to the cycle of continuous learning (see Chapter 10). The emphasis will be on the accuracy and immediacy of an organization's 'learning experiences'. We can expect Information Technology to truly deliver its much heralded promise to move the company closer to its customers, suppliers and the creative input of its knowledge workers. Understanding and exploiting the information will be the key competitive differentiator; technology, as always, will remain simply the channel. In order to maximize the benefits of this knowledge economy, organizations will have to become more proficient at creating and sustaining relationships. Customers will only be willing to divulge their preferences and desires if they feel they can get something valuable in return – a more personalized, competitively priced service, for example. 'Employees' (working within whatever formal/informal/psychological/financial constructs there may be in the future) will only be willing to give up their knowledge and expertise when they feel motivated and supported in doing so. Organizations will need to come up with different ways of engendering loyalty and a sense of community. We can also expect that they become comfortable with the organic, biological, self-managing new physics-based models of change. Already, Visa is a blueprint for this. There the member banks send representatives to a system of national, regional, and international boards. While the system appears to be hierarchical, the Visa hierarchy is not a chain of command. Instead, each board serves as a forum for members to raise common issues, debate them, and reach consensus and resolution. Dee Hock, the CEO responsible for creating Visa in this way, drew his inspiration from living cells, brains, immune systems and ant colonies as much as from modern organizational and governmental models. The trick, he says, is to find the right balance that allows the system to avoid turf fights and back-stabbing on the one hand, and authoritarian micromanagement on the other. 'Neither competition nor co-operation can rise to its highest potential unless both are seamlessly blended', says Hock. 'Either without the other swiftly becomes dangerous and destructive.'

At the level of the individual, change will be something that is increasingly chosen by the individual as a way of maintaining employability; self-directed learning rather than company-imposed training will be the norm. Expect to see a continued power shift from companies offering jobs to individuals offering expertise; from hired hands to hired guns. To survive and thrive in such a market, individuals will need to work not just on their technical capabilities but also on their self-esteem, self-awareness, change-resilience, marketing and PR. At the same time, a company of mercenaries will be a soulless place, and one not conducive to the synergistic sharing of knowledge that future corporations like Visa depend on. So the most successful Smart New Careerists will not only be able to demonstrate competence, confidence and creativity, but also community. The ability to connect with others – however brief the contract – will be a key differentiator in the marketplace.

It will be a brave new world, but only for the brave.

Which brings us to ...

12

Awareness, Alignment, Change and You

FIFTEEN PRECEPTS FOR THE SMART CHANGE MASTER

'I came to realise that there was no certainty any more in human things, and [that] a search for meaning had to move up our agendas if we were not to be caught hanging around waiting for some mythical leader to tell us where to go and how to get there.'

Charles Handy

At the heart of this book is an understanding that change never happens in organizations unless people change. The extent to which change in organizations is painful, protracted, costly and resisted is the extent to which individuals conspire to create that reality in what they think, what they say and what they do. It's as simple as that; there is no other way.

This chapter sums up fifteen things you might help yourself to remember about life, change and the whole damn thing. There is no need to behave like the tribe. And I guess by virtue of you reading this far, you are determined not to do so.

But first, let me remind you of the two extremely simple messages of this book, because each of them can be applied to your own life and career.

Change takes:

Awareness

- know what you want

- know where you are

Alignment

- change your behaviors, your systems and your attitudes until they are in alignment with what you want

- maintain awareness of what is happening around you so that you can continuously adjust your behavior

- work with what works; learn from and discard what doesn't.

All the rest is detail ...

And now, those fifteen change precepts:

Precept 1

You must learn to handle frustration. If you're not frustrated, you're probably not trying hard enough or dreaming big enough. Any great success is accompanied by great frustration – or, rather, great frustration managed correctly. How many times do we have to tell ourselves stories like that of Edison (who when he had finally invented a working light bulb after 100 attempts, told his audience, astonished at his perseverance, that he had never failed, but merely discovered 99 ways *not* to invent a working light bulb) to accept that this is true. This precept, like so many others, is about learning how to change ourselves. Our instinct for a pain- (frustration-) free life leads us to subdue our ambitions, to aim low. Fight it.

Smart quotes

'A two-step formula for handling stress. Step 1: Don't sweat the small stuff. Step 2: It's all small stuff.'

Anthony Robbins

Precept 2

You must learn to reframe things that bring you pain. Mistakes, for example, (which you'll be making plenty of as a consequence of Precept 1) are not, in that beautiful phrase, 'the birthplace of regret' – *unless that's how you want to perceive them*. They do – or can –

- allow learning to happen

- encourage spontaneity in providing you with more chances to put things right (whereas always getting things right would be tiresome)

- supply warnings that you were not thinking or acting with enough clarity and focus

- provide a test of your capacity for taking responsibility for the outcomes of your actions.

Reframing is not about positive thinking but about giving yourself a new way forward. Each of the above interpretations or 'frames' is constructive rather than destructive. If you choose to frame mistakes as a sign that you are stupid, then not only have you come to a dead end about yourself, you are going to feel pretty shitty about attempting the next challenge.

Precept 3

You must learn to handle criticism. Change threatens people and they can often defend themselves by attacking you. If you sense that you are really being criticized in an unhelpful way rather than receiving interesting feedback (which is one way to frame any criticism), then here are eight ways to respond (from a fine book on erasing feelings of guilt, *Healing the Shame that Binds You* by John Bradshaw):

- *Clarifying.* 'what exactly in me is causing you to say that?'

- *Confronting.* 'I need to let you know how your comments make me feel'

- *Columboing.* 'Tell me again ...; did you mean ...; let me ask you one more question ...'

- *Confessing.* 'I take full responsibility for my actions. Here's what I'm going to do ...'

- *Confirming.* 'I agree with some of what you say; I also think that I have these positive qualities ...'

- *Comforting.* 'Good point; I've let you down. How can I help you by putting things right?'

- *Confusing.* Which is a bizarre technique that I've used only in my imagination but maybe you're more daring than me. *Confusing* is about having fun rather than being defensive; you deliberately say an irrelevant word that perplexes them, and, in the delay leave or change the subject, e.g. 'Boy, the traffic was otiose today!'

Precept 4

You must learn to deal with adversity and failure. When it happens, remember your purpose, your reason for doing all this and put this small set back in the context of the bigger scheme. Allow yourself to feel bad before reframing; you wouldn't put a cap on your peaks, so don't cut off your capacity for feeling other, less positive emotions. Always be interested in your failures, not so that you can wallow in self-recrimination, but to seek a better understanding of what went 'wrong'.

Smart quotes

'How to live in non-stop change

- figure out what is actually changing
- decide what is really over for you and let go of it
- distinguish between current losses and your memories of old wounds
- identify your continuities – what about your life is solid amidst change?
- take time out to relax and renew yourself
- look at yourself creatively, as a process and not a product
- experiment a little every day
- learn.'

Adapted from *Managing Transitions* by William Bridges

Precept 5

Always seek ways to increase your own capacity for being a positive role model for others.

Precept 6

Know when it's time to make a change. Here are two signs to look out for.

- It's time for a change when you have **disengaged** – when you are no longer committed to a purpose or goal, team or project. It is madness to put up with a situation when it no longer motivates or inspires, when you are just doing it out of habit, for the money or because you can't be bothered to change. If you become disengaged, you will produce an environment which will only ever support your mindset. Others will disengage from you; the work will lose its meaning and you will find yourself lonely and isolated. Situations like this rarely improve with time. Get out quick.

- It's time for a change when you are **disoriented** – when nothing seems to bring you satisfaction, where every effort you make to improve things seems only to bring forth three more problems. When you have become confused over the point of a job, a relationship or a direction you set for yourself previously, it's rare for the purpose to return of its own accord. Get clear quick.

Precept 7

Be your own best ally: support yourself well in making a change. Here are four ways:

- Change thrives on congruence between thought, word and deed. Check that your thoughts are positive and constructive and you speak well of yourself and your change efforts.

- Change thrives on repetition. Practice the changed behavior or habit, again and again. Write it in your personal organizer; treat the change like a business schedule; pay attention to it, make time for it.

- Change thrives on inner conditioning; give your mind a motivating goal by imagining your self having changed. Give it something to move away from by listing the downsides and perils of not changing.

- Ask for help. Such behavior is a sign of strength, not weakness.

Precept 8

Sort out what's important about your work. Do you have a vision? Do you stand for a cause? What are you doing all this for? No, it's not obvious, and even if it seems obvious to you now, you'll probably forget it further down the road. Get a purpose, get a life. And remember that money is a marvelous necessary thing, because it allows you to do other, better things with it. But having money as your purpose is a mistake, because it means that everything else you do will have to align behind that purpose to make it happen. And in reality, maybe only 5% of the pain you will ever feel in your career will be over money.

Here's some good advice:

Shaping your career on purpose

Use this formula for a good career decision. Over the years, I've devised a very simple formula that lays out the critical factors to consider when you're making a career choice: T + P + E × V.

T stands for talent, and it's where you should begin when you're considering a career choice or a career change. Very simply, the questions are, What are your strengths and weaknesses? How can you focus on your strengths and manage your weaknesses?

Most people aren't using their talents. They didn't choose their career; their career chose them. They got into a line of work because they had to get a job, or somebody told them they'd be good at a job. They were young, they started down a certain path, and they never stopped to ask what their calling might be – not just their job, but their real calling. Then, before they know it, they hit midlife, and they're asking themselves, 'Why am I doing this? Why did I start down this path instead of following my real talents?'

P stands for passion, or for purpose. Talents develop best in the context of interest. Aristotle said it a long time ago: 'Where the needs of the world and your talents cross, there lies your vocation.' Ask yourself, 'What needs doing in your organization? What needs doing in the world?' Then put your talents to work on some area of need that you believe in. Choosing your work is your chance to do something more meaningful than getting up in the morning, putting in your time, doing what it takes to pay the bills.

'The E stands for environment: What work environment best suits your style, your temperament, your values? I often meet people who have identified their talents and their passion, but who are working in an environment that doesn't permit them to express themselves. When they move to a new environment, one that uses their talents and honors their values, they suddenly find an alignment that works. They discover new energy and new purpose in their work.

> 'V stands for vision – how you see the rest of your life. Talent, purpose, and environment are all about work style and work choice. Vision describes how work fits into the rest of your life. Where do you want to live? How much money is enough? How important are your relationships? What are you doing to stay healthy?'
>
> Interview with Richard Leider, author of *The Power of Purpose* (Berrett-Koehler, 1997) , *Fast Company* magazine, Issue 13

Precept 9

Don't waste your time doing anything which is not in alignment with your vision or purpose. You don't have much time. Doing things which are not in alignment saps your energy and creates fragmentation and lack of focus in your actions.

There's always somebody around in an organization who is 'only there for the money'. Because they're 'only there for the money' all they have to do is 'just be there'. So let them waste their time. Most meetings, for example, are a waste of time not because they don't have a purpose, but because people *behave* as if the meetings don't have a purpose. Don't join in.

Precept 10

Do something every day to keep the learning cycle spinning. What questions are you being curious about? How are you nurturing your creativity? How are you pushing yourself to take risks? Are you sure?

Precept 11

Challenge the status quo.

Precept 12

Break the rules – both at banal and transformational levels. Andy Law has some ideas.

Precept 13

Be on the lookout for making change. At the end of every month (or week if yours is a particularly fast-moving place), draw up a list of three things that your organization needs to learn to do better. Only cross off the ones from last time that are unequivocally being addressed successfully. After six months, see how much the list has changed.

Carry out a similar exercise with a friendly customer and/or supplier. This is not just about improving service but about enlisting their (free) advice on improving your company.

Precept 14

You exist, it could be said, as a result of who you are in relation to your own and other people's perspectives. You are a function of your network of intimates, friends, colleagues, teachers. Ask yourself: whose perspective

Smart quotes

'In all this talk, where is the self? The answer is nowhere, because the self is not a thing, but as Jerome Brunner says, 'a point of view that unifies the flow of experience into a coherent narrative' – a narrative striving to connect with other narratives and become richer.'

From *Communities of Commitment*, essay by Peter Senge and Fred Kofman in *Learning Organizations*

would I really like to open myself up to? What is the nature and quality of my relationships? What do they teach me? How many challenge me? How could I open myself – even if only temporarily – to a new perspective? If organizations need 'deep change' to truly change, what does deep change mean to me? When have I experienced it? When might I avoid it?

Precept 15

Finally, remember once more that organizations don't change, people do. So this book draws to a close by once again focusing on the individual human being in change. And the advice?

'Know thyself.'

Be interested in and observant of the factors that make you a good change agent. What happens inside you when you are confronted by significant change – what emotions do you go through and in what order? What are the physical and behavioral signs? What does it actually feel like when you become committed to a cause? What, exactly, makes you frustrated? Observing these changes in your own experience will make you more effective at observing and empathizing with those of others. Watch keenly what others do when they go through change. Reflect. Theorize. Keep a diary, perhaps. (See *Diary of a Change Agent*, Tony Page, Gower 1998.)

... or write a book.

'To accomplish great things, we must not only act, but also dream; not only plan, but also believe.'

Anatole France

Index